THE LAST WITNESS

The Memoirs of George L. Mabry, Jr. from D-Day to the Battle of the Bulge

by Stephen Cano

Contents

For George, Abigail and Benny

George L. Mabry D-Day Photo

Foreword

The bloody and deadly Battle of the Hurtgen Forest produced four Medal of Honor recipients from the Eight Infantry Regiment of the Fourth Infantry Division. One of those was Pedro Cano. Stephen Cano has written an excellent book, Unsung Hero – Private *Pedro Cano*, about the bravery and valor of his uncle Pedro Cano. Stephen not only wrote of the heroic deeds of Pedro but also how the Department of the Army, with what seemed bigotry and prejudice, treated Pedro Cano's valor award. However, Pedro's home town and the American Legion rallied to have his Distinguished Service Cross appropriately presented and later the award was rightfully upgraded to the Medal of Honor.

Stephen has now written this book on another of the Hurtgen Forest Medal of Honor recipients, George L Mabry, Jr., my father. Dad was a man of action whether leading soldiers in front of his battalion to seize a critical bridge on Utah Beach, assaulting a German machine gun position, or making his way alone through wire and mines to charge German bunkers in the Hurtgen Forest. George Mabry never hesitated. He took action when action was needed.

Mabry's creed his entire life was to never ask anyone to do what he would not willingly do himself. This ran the gamut from cleaning toilets to charging the enemy and extended into everything he did in his life.

As a general officer flying from Panama Canal Zone to the US, an overhead light fixture came loose during takeoff, fell and hit a flight attendant causing a gash in the attendant's head. Without hesitation, Mabry immediately rendered first aid to the attendant while all other passengers watched. After applying a pressure bandage to stop the bleeding, the airline captain came back and asked, "Doctor, will she be alright?" The man of action, Mabry, replied, "I'm not a doctor but she should get medical treatment when we land."

While at the Fort McNair Officer's Club pool, George Mabry was sitting pool side with his family when he suddenly leaped to his bare feet and climbed the eight-foot chain linked fence that surrounded the pool and ran one hundred yards to a playground. He had been watching two young children playing on a seesaw when one fell. Mabry immediately saw the child was injured and ran to her aid. While he comforted the young girl, who had broken her arm, he yelled to the lifeguards to call an ambulance and notify the parents. Meanwhile, the others at the pool stood at the fence and watched.

During one of his tours in the Pentagon when required to wear civilian clothes and not a uniform, Mabry was driving home to Falls Church, Virginia on a snowy day. As he passed a wooded lot, his car was pelted by snowballs. Most adults would have been upset but not Mabry. He drove past the lot and parked, gathered an arm full of snowballs, and sneaked up on the boys throwing snowballs. Mabry let his snowballs fly. What ensued was a great snowball fight with Mabry and the teenage boys having grand time. The man of action was always willing to have fun. Mabry also never took himself too seriously.

The Army's formal uniform, the mess dress, requires miniature medals to be worn on the jacket. However, since there is no miniature for the Medal of Honor, it is worn on the blue ribbon around the neck. At a formal dance Mabry was greeting guests in a receiving line, when a young Army captain's wife, after being introduced to the commanding general, took hold of the Medal of Honor and asked, "What's this?". Mabry quickly replied, "You can't find these anymore but they used to be in Crackerjack boxes." Not stopping the young lady turned to her husband and asked him, "Why don't you have one of those?" The completely mortified captain was put at ease by a chuckling Mabry and the receiving line continued. George Mabry was not only a man of action but a man of compassion, kindness and honor.

Dad was only 5'7" tall and the nicest person you would ever meet. Nothing like Rambo or any of the Hollywood fiction characters. Dad was a story teller and had a marvelous sense of humor. He was also a magnificent public speaker and was always in demand. I had to change my wedding date because he had a speaking engagement on the date my wife had chosen. And my dad was the best man. I remember once he was invited to Ft Benning's Infantry School as a guest speaker along with about five other combat vets to discuss war experiences. The school rotated students through classrooms where the vets were speaking. The speakers gave about four presentations throughout the day. Dad was so riveting and funny his last two speeches were for a standing room crowd only. Soldiers and faculty kept coming back. His jokes were always about himself and his experiences. He was laid back and never took himself too seriously. Young children were fascinated by him. He would play and entertain my kids for hours. I could tell you stories about him for days. Dad commissioned me and as an adult he became my best friend. After he retired, he and I would hunt and fish together anytime I could get some leave and get home.

—George L. Mabry III

Preparing for War

On June 1, 1940, I graduated from Presbyterian College and received a commission as a second lieutenant in the United States Army Reserve as a result of having participated in the Reserve Officers Training Program at Presbyterian College for four years. Prior to graduation, I had signed a contract to teach and coach baseball at a high school in North Carolina during the second term of 1941 and also negotiated a contract to play baseball during the summer of 1941 with the team in the Blue Ridge League. At the same time, I had become concerned about the saber-rattling Adolf Hitler was engaged in in Germany and could detect the formation of war clouds gathering over Europe. So, without much persuasion, I also applied to go on active duty with the regular United States Army under the newly created Thomason Act. This Act authorized the selection of a number of qualified reserve officers to go on active competitive duty with the regular army for a period of one year provided those officers selected would sign a contract to remain on unmarried during that one year of duty. Additionally, after the one year of competitive active duty terminated, a small group of these officers would be offered commissions in the regular army. This sounded like a good challenge so I applied. As luck would have it, my application was approved and I received orders to report on July 5, 1940 to the 8th Infantry Regiment of the Fourth Infantry Division stationed at Fort Benning, Ga. Based on these orders, I quickly requested and obtained releases from the contracts I had signed to teach, coach, and play baseball in North Carolina during the year 1941. Upon rereading my Army orders, I noted that one Walter B. Todd, a 1939 graduate of Presbyterian College, was also listed to report to the 8th Infantry Regiment on the same day as I had been ordered to report. Since I knew Walt, and he owned an automobile and lived in Clinton, South Carolina, I contacted Walt and we joined forces for a journey to Fort Benning, Ga.

The trip to Fort Benning was rather uneventful but things picked up when we arrived. The 8th Infantry Regiment was located at tent city, the old Hominy Church area of Fort Benning, Ga. After spending over an hour and a half walking up and down dirty company streets which were bordered on each side with countless number of canvas tents set up on wooden tent frames, we spied a very distinguished looking man who was about 6 ft. 3 in. tall. He had gray hair. His uniform was immaculate and his carriage was erect as a ramrod as he strolled along twirling a riding crop. We just knew he must be a general officer and should not be trifled with but we were so desperate to locate the regimental headquarters of the 8th Infantry Regiment. We approached this gentleman with a, "Sir, could you tell us where the regimental headquarters is located?" To our utter amazement, he turned out to be the sergeant major, Grace, the sergeant major of the 8th Infantry Regiment. He not only escorted us to regimental headquarters, but also ushered us directly into the regimental adjutant's office where we received our specific assignment from Major Rothmick, who was the regimental adjutant. The specific assignment assigned us to Company B of the First Battalion, 8th Infantry.

Having gotten over one hurdle, our spirits had begun to rise, but unbeknown to us, they would soon be dashed against the rocks. Walter and I were wearing civilian clothes because Walt had only one regulation khaki uniform which he was saving for his first day of duty with the regular army. I had about three uniforms, but did not want to upstage Walt. As we approached the endless rows of tents and Company B, First Battalion, 8th infantry, our pace slowed due to the many ill clothed people we saw dashing around the company area in great haste. Many wore uniforms but others were bare headed and dressed in ragged civilian coveralls and were bare footed. However, all of them were dashing into company tents carrying various item of military clothing, footwear and equipment like backpacks, mess kits and shelter halves. We rightly assumed these men were new recruits who had just begun to draw their military clothing and equipment from the supply room. Walter and I located the tent on which was a rough sign which read in big bold letters, "Company Commander, "and underneath it, in much smaller letters, "First Sergeant." So, we walked in, and sitting behind the desk was a slightly built man who appeared to be somewhat nervous and as we introduced ourselves, we told this individual that we were second lieutenants reporting to active duty. He then immediately jumped up and asked us to step outside the tent.

Once outside, he told us that the commander was a rather tough man and recommended that when we went in to see the company commander, that we should be especially polite and demonstrate military bearing of the highest order. We thanked him very much and stepped back into the tent. Now this tent had been divided with a partition and a small door. So, we tapped on the door and a booming voice said, "Come in." We went in and sitting behind the desk was a man about 6 ft. 2 in. tall, dark complected with a hooked nose. So, Walt and I reported for duty. Now this gentleman stood up and stretched himself to his full height, looking down his nose at us and said, "Well, I'm glad to see some people who've come to help me. Now, the first question is where are your uniforms?" Walt said, "Sir, we do not have uniforms yet."

"Well, starting right now, before tomorrow morning, each of you will have six shirts, six pairs of trousers, three pairs of boots and three hats. Now the quartermaster sales store is closed, so don't you ask me how to get them. But you better be damn sure you have them by tomorrow morning at reveille (wake up time or bugle call). He turned to Walt and said, "You meet reveille in the morning," and to me, "You meet reveille the next morning, and alternate thereafter." He turned to Walt again and said, "You are hereby the supply officer." He turned to me and said, "You are hereby the mess officer. Are there any questions?" Naturally, we said, "No sir." He said, "Dismissed."

We left the tent rather reeling under these directions because we really didn't know what he was talking about. We wandered over to the tent that had been assigned to us as quarters. The tent was on a tent frame. Outside the tent was a little wooden frame in which there was a military helmet and that was our wash basin. We had two cots inside the tent. So, Walter and I went inside the tent and before we got settled, sat down at our respective cots and started thinking about these directions the company commander had given us. We figured out that reveille meant *early* the next morning and supply officer meant he had responsibility of supplies and I was responsible for running the place where soldiers ate. Walter and I thought that maybe we should get the first sergeant over and ask some questions about the company commander because it appeared the company commander was a very tough individual.

We walked over and asked the first sergeant to come visit us later in the evening. The first sergeant came over and we asked him to come in. He came in, standing at perfect attention. We said, "first sergeant, have a seat." He said, "Sirs, I'd prefer to stand." We said, "Well sergeant, we just want to talk to you and ask you a few questions about the company commander. For example, what are some of the company commander's idiosyncrasies?" The first sergeant, standing at perfect attention said, "Sirs, he has none." "Well sergeant, what kind of man is he? Can you give us some opinions of what he's like?" "I'd prefer not to sir." Finally, Walt said, "Well, first sergeant, what do the men call the company commander?" The first sergeant, still standing at attention said, "Sirs, request permission to be excused a moment." We said, Permission granted." He turned on his heels, walked out of the tent, came back in, and standing at perfect attention again, leaned over, and behind his hand said, "Sirs, they call him the Iron Duke." Well that was enough for us. We thanked the first sergeant and excused him.

The next morning, bright and early, before daylight in fact, the reveille bugle was sounded. So, Walt dashed out to take reveille and I prepared to go over to the mess hall and start what I thought would be my duties. Walt had one uniform and I had three so we didn't have to go get them the previous night. We didn't tell the company commander about that. So, I jaunted over to the mess hall. The troops had begun to line up to go in the mess hall and each had a mess kit which consisted of an aluminum kit with a lid and a knife, fork and spoon. I began to inspect the utensils of the soldiers who were lined up. Many of them were in civilian clothes, ill-fitting and ragged civilian clothes, some barefooted. I began to look at the utensils and all of a sudden behind me appeared the company commander. Fortunately, an old soldier saw the company commander and called, "Attention," in a very loud voice and everybody snapped to. The company commander gave everybody, "At ease," and then approached me and said, "I see you're inspecting the mess kits." I said, "Yes sir." He said, "Let me show you how to inspect them." So, he took over and reached over and took the knife, fork, and spoon from a recruit that was barefooted and had some rather long hair. He took the knife and scraped the fork and said, "Soldier, what is that?" The soldier said, "Sir, it looks like egg." He said, "It doesn't look like egg, dammit, it is egg. Get in the rear of the line." Another soldier was standing there and his hair was hanging down on his forehead and he was a new recruit. The company commander reached up and snatched on that bit of hair and said, "Soldier, you've got to get a haircut. Get in the rear of the line." Well, this continued until he demonstrated to me how detailed he wanted me to inspect not only the eating utensils of the soldiers but their dress and appearance every morning before they entered the mess hall. Having gotten over this hurdle, we then put on our full field packs according to a directive that was posted on the bulletin board and went to the company street for a company formation.

The first sergeant lined up the company. The platoon sergeants had taken charge of course, and then the first sergeant turned over the company to the company commander at which time we the platoon leaders took charge of our respective platoons. The company commander incidentally was a veteran of World War I and had a head injury as a result of combat and periodically his left eye would automatically close. On occasion, he would push that left eye open with his hand or finger. When he got all of us in formation, he said, "Everybody display your dog tags." Now the dog tag is an identification tag that you wore around your neck. Second, he asked, "Does everyone have a full canteen of water?" One soldier released his hand indicating that he did not have a full canteen of water. So, the company commander said, "Run and get a full canteen of water and report back immediately," which this soldier did. The company commander then directed the platoon leaders to inspect and confirm if everyone had their dog tags, identification tags, which we did and reported accordingly. When that was finished, the company commander said, "Right face. Follow me." And we took off on a hike.

Now no one knew what we were going to do on that particular morning, but it became quite obvious by this time that we were going on a hike in the deep sands of Georgia on this hot sixth day of July to test our stamina. Fortunately, I had been playing baseball and as in excellent physical condition. Now the platoon leaders were not permitted to march at the head of their platoons. They were to march at the rear end of their platoons and the platoon sergeant was to march behind the platoon leader. That's because the head of a column, when it's marching, takes longer steps and the tail of a column has to run to catch up, to keep up on occasion. So, the officers were always placed in that position to be sure that they understood how the rear of the column was marching.

We had not gone over 2 miles, when the platoon sergeant, Sergeant Stokes, came up behind me and said, "Lieutenant, do not look around. Don't let the company commander know that I'm talking to you but I like the cut of your jib. Let me give you a piece of advice. No matter how hot and tired you get, do not take a sip of that water in your canteen. In fact, if you're so dry and dusty, when you fart you spot your drawers, still do not take a drop of that water."

Under my breath, I thanked him. "Thank you very much, sergeant," and kept walking. We continued to march for about nine to ten miles. At each ten-minute break after each hour of marching, I would not touch one drop of water. Finally, the company turned us around and we marched back to the company street. Now we had several stragglers, but the company commander waited until every last member of that company had reached the company street.

Then he announced in a very loud voice that he wanted the company to form a big circle. Having done that, he told us to remove our canteens from our canteen covers, unscrew the tops thereof, which we did. Then he said, "When I count to three, I want everyone to turn the canteen upside down." On the count of three every man turned his canteen upside down. As the water ran out of the individual's respective canteen, he would say, "Get over here." So, the first ones that ran out of water were in one group. The second group had a little more water left in the canteen than the first group. Then the third group had the most water left in their canteen. When it ended up, fortunately my canteen was still running. This surprised the company commander, so he told me to take charge of the group that had run out of water first, to form a big circle with them, make them put on their masks, put their rifles above their heads and run in a circle until he said stop. I acknowledged the order and organized this group in a circle. I put on my gas mask too and I put my rifle above my head and we ran. Finally, one man hit the ground, passed out. A second man hit the ground and passed out. When the third man hit the ground and passed out, he hollered to me and said, "That is enough." Now what he was to demonstrate here was water discipline. In those days, you were supposed to be able to live on one canteen of water for a full day and night and have enough left to shave the following morning. In later years the military permitted drinking as much water as needed and encouraged soldiers to do so. But in those days, we practiced what is known as water discipline. This is what he was trying to get over to us. Well, he made a point, a very strong point with those who were subjected to this type of treatment. I ran with them because if they were going to run, I was going to demonstrate that I could do it too. I was in charge of that group and whatever they were suppose to do, I was going to do it too.

Earlier, it appears I concentrated on the height of people. For example, Sergeant Major Grace, he was a tall, distinguished looking man. And Carl Duffner was 6 ft. 2 in. Later I'll talk about Major Bull Holland from Texas who was our battalion commander. He was 6 ft. 4 in. tall. It just appears to me that for many years every individual I ever ran into of authority were always big and tall when I was short of stature. It did not bother me. I was 5 ft. 7 and ¼ in. and I always emphasize that quarter of an inch. But I didn't think that I had the little man's complex but I was aware that the big man has an advantage over the little man. This goes back to football in college. For example, in our day everybody fell out to try out for football. What do coaches do? They look at the big men and say, "What position do you play?" Then to the next bigger men they say, "What position are you out for?" Then when they come to the little fellows, they say, "Why are you out here boy?" So, it's just normal to look at the big men because theoretically he's supposed to be tougher and stronger and have more endurance. But that is not necessarily true at all times. All my life, I think I've had to put out a little more, so to speak, than the big man, particularly in athletics, in order to be recognized and make the team. I did go to school on an athletic scholarship. Principally, it was a baseball scholarship, but I also played football for two years. However, I was so light, only about 145 lbs. I didn't fare very well playing on the football team playing against Georgia Tech, the University of South Carolina and the University of Tennessee, where their line had 240 lb. tackles. I was playing guard and I was 145 pounds. But baseball, I did very well. So, I felt that in a leadership position, and I still feel this way, that particularly when you are dealing with troops and if you are going to issue them an order, you better be prepared to do exactly what you expect them to do. And later in life, I coined the phrase that I think is very appropriate and applicable: never ask anyone to do anything that you would not willingly do yourself. If I asked anybody to do something, I would do it along with them.

Earlier I spoke about my company commander, the iron Duke. Well, his real name was Capt. Carl the iron Duke Duffner. And incidentally, the company commander of C Company was Captain Charles Buck Lanham, and he was a very articulate individual and he called the iron Duke the iron head. Capt. Lanham became a general officer and even though he left the Fourth Division in about 1940-1941, he returned during World War II and commanded the 22nd Infantry Regiment and made quite a name for himself.

One evening while walking down through the Battalion area, I saw a large group of individuals gathered around what appeared to be two or three people on the ground, so I assumed that a fight was ongoing. As I approached the group, a man on the ground was thrashing around a great deal and it appeared that two to three other men were trying to hold him down. I couldn't understand what was going on, but about this time a sergeant walked up and said, "Lieutenant, I can take care of that man if you just ask everyone to stand back," which I did, and told the sergeant to take charge. The sergeant immediately directed everyone who was trying to restrain this individual to turn him loose. The individual on the ground continued having convulsions, which I had never seen before. After this sergeant approached this individual, he reached down, picked up a stick and forced this man's mouth open and placed the stick between his teeth and told everyone to be quiet and just stand by. Soon the convulsions in this individual began to subside, so I asked the sergeant, "What was this man's ailment?" He said, "Oh Lieutenant, he's just having a fit. Well, later I realized that this individual was having an epileptic fit, or epileptic seizure, but it was something new to me. The point of the story is that I found that in the military, particularly in the Army in my experience, there's always someone who knows what to do in a given situation, and if you let that individual take charge, usually he knows what to do and everything will turn out all right.

In Company F was a corporal by the name of Corporal Green. Now Corporal Green was a combination of several men. He was a very religious man, but not overbearing. In other words, he did not try to convert anyone to his religious beliefs but he on occasion would preach at local churches in the Georgia area. He was also the company barber and would cut hair of the individual members of the company after duty hours for a very nominal fee. As I recall, it was about ten cents. In addition to this, he was an excellent instructor and a real expert marksman with the rifle. I recall him very well.

One day, Captain Duffner, being a rather senior individual, senior captain, in fact he'd been a captain for ten years, was a senior officer in the Battalion because the battalion commander, Major Bull Holland, had gone on a trip someplace for professional reasons. And the Battalion had scheduled for that afternoon a Battalion parade. Now Captain Duffner was really feeling his oats. Here he was going to be the Battalion commander in this particular Battalion parade. So, he stationed himself very early out in the Battalion area where he could watch the companies begin to form in order to march to the parade field. While standing there, and many members of the Battalion were milling around getting prepared to fall into company formations, a Lieutenant Heymer, who was the officer of the day, began to walk down through the Battalion area. Now Lieutenant Heymer had the bizzard on his arm that indicated in white letters on his black band so to speak, "OD," meaning officer of the day, so this could be discerned quite a distance away. And he was about 200 yards from where Captain Duffner was standing. Well, Captain Duffner wanted to make a point. So, he began hollering, "LIETENANT, LIEUTENANT OFFICER OF THE DAY." And other people along the line picked it up and said, "Lieutenant Heymer, Lieutenant Heymer, He's talking to you." Lieutenant Heymer stopped and said, "YES SIR." Captain Duffner says, "IS IT NOT CUSTOMARY THAT WHEN YOU PASS A SENIOR OFFICER THAT YOU SALUTE?" "YES SIR." Heymar says. Capt. Duffner says, "WELL DAMMIT, SALUTE!" Lieutenant Heymer saluted, "YES SIR," and began to move on. Again, Captain Duffner hollers, "LIEUTENANT, LIEUTENANT OFFICER OF THE DAY." The word was passed again, "Lieutenant Heymer, he's talking to you again." Heymer stops again, stands at attention and says, "YES SIR." Capt. Duffner then says, 'IS IT NOT CUSTOMARY THAT YOU, WHEN YOU TERMINATE A CONVERSATION WITH A SENIOR OFFICER, THAT YOU SALUTE?" "YES SIR," says Heymer. "WELL DAMMIT, SALUTE!" says Duffner. Heymer salutes and then moves on. Well, for the next two or three weeks, Lieutenant Heymer, when he walked around anywhere in the regimental area, was always very alert looking for Capt. Duffner. Now Capt. Duffner I think had a couple of points in mind when he did this. First, he considered himself a very strict disciplinarian. And on this particular occasion, he wanted to demonstrate to everyone in that Battalion that he expected to be saluted as far as any man in that Battalion could see him. And he made his point loud and clear with that one demonstration.

Major Davis, a native of Georgia, assumed command. Major Davis was a real crusty, tough individual. In October, we had begun to move the troops from tents into wooden barracks. The officers had not had a building constructed for them to occupy as yet. Therefore, the officers were still living in tents. So, the officers were living in tents in a small area clustered together. We had only one shower house facility. It was a small house, that shower house. It had two shower stalls in it and about six lavatories where one could shave, etc. In October, it had begun to get a little cool at Fort Benning. On this particular day, I thought I had gotten off work real early. This is about 5:30 in the afternoon. So maybe I was going to pull the officer's day duty, but anyway I rushed to my tent, took off my clothes and got a robe with soap and towel and dashed up to the shower house hoping to get a shower rather quickly. And as I walked into the shower house, I noted one of the shower stalls being occupied by a Captain Larrifeld, who commanded G Company, and he was an older man than I, so I spoke to him and he spoke to me. So, I immediately jumped in the other shower stall and was feeling very lucky and had soaped myself down really good. And I was just about to turn on the shower again and enjoy my bath when all of a sudden, the door to the shower house opened and in stepped Major Davis. And he had a habit of clearing his throat on occasion when he wanted someone's attention. So, he cleared his throat (ahem...ahem). So, I stuck my head out of the shower stall and said, "good evening Major Davis." And he says, "good evening. It is customary that when I come in this shower house, I get a shower." And I said, oh, yes sir," and then it hit me. It appeared that he was implying that I should offer him my shower stall immediately. So, I said, "Sir, would you like this shower stall?" He said, "indeed I would." So, he made me step outside and I still in the cold, soap completely covering me, standing there shivering while he, inside the shower, taking a nice warm shower and mumbling to himself, humming to himself and clearing his throat on occasion.

Another morning, Major Davis and I were in this little famous shower house shaving and naturally, I wasn't saying anything, but just standing there shaving, because I never said anything unless Major Davis brought up a subject. We were shaving along when all of a sudden, the band struck up some music up in the Battalion area. I heard it but paid no attention to it. All of a sudden Major Davis slammed his razor down on the wooden shelf, then took his hand and hammered down on the shelf while looking at me and hollered, "do you hear what I hear?" I, having jumped 5 ft., settled down and said, "Sir, I don't know. What do you hear?" He says, "listen to that music that the band is playing." And I said, "yes sir." He said, "go get that bandmaster and bring him to me immediately." So, I said, "yes sir," and dashed out of the shower house with only a T-shirt on with lather all over my face and started running up to the bandmaster. I tried to get the warrant officer's attention. Finally, some soldier in the front ranks stopped blowing a horn and said, "Mr. Cannette, "I think that was his name, pointed toward me and the warrant officer turned around and I beckoned for him to come to me. I told him that Major Davis said to bring him to Major Davis immediately. So, the bandmaster said, "wait till I finish this piece." I said, "Not on your life. He said now. " So, he turned the band over to his second sergeant, second in command, and we charged down towards the shower house. The bandmaster (also a warrant officer) asked me, "what is the problem?" I said, "I have no idea, but you better believe that Major Davis is really upset." We walked into the shower house and major Davis was standing there with his hands on his hips and lather on his face and foaming at the mouth, more or less. When the bandmaster stood at attention, Major Davis says, "what in the hell are you playing that piece for?" And the bandmaster said, "Sir, I don't know what you mean." The bandmaster continued, "let me explain, Major Davis. I found a sheet of music. The title was torn off, and I was playing that." Major Davis said, "my God, man, don't you know what you're playing?" He said, "no sir, I do not." Major Davis said, "you are playing *Marching Through Georgia*." From then on, he gave the bandmaster a lacing that lasted for 20 minutes. Well, I'll tell you this. That bandmaster, from then on, knew what sheet of music he was playing.

Another thing that Major Davis did, he delighted in doing, and this happened on one occasion that I remember very vividly. I was with F Company out on a road march. We'd been marching for an hour or so and I was at the head of the column, being the company commander. And Major Davis approached the company in his command car, and approached it from the head of the column, in other words, meeting me. And when he got opposite where I was marching, he stopped the command car. The command car was a vehicle that had curtains on in the wintertime and opened during the summer, tall wheels and had a running board, one of these old-style command cars. And that's about the best description I can give you. So, I naturally went over and reported to him. And he said, "Get in, lieutenant." And I got in the back seat with them and naturally, he had a driver. So, we started down the road going the opposite direction of where my company was marching. After we passed the tail of the company, Major Davis turned to me and said, "you know, I have been tried for kicking two second lieutenants in the butt." And I said, "oh, is that right sir?" And he kept talking like this, impressing upon me how rough he was and that he should not be trifled with. Well, he continued talking to me until we had gotten at least 2 miles down the road. Finally, he told the driver to stop, and turned to me and said, "Lieutenant, do you and I understand each other?" And I said, "yes sir, indeed I understand you perfectly." So, I rendered a salute and took off. I immediately started running to catch up wit my company, because I had detected that Major Davis was trying me. So, I jogged pretty fast. Finally, I reached the tail of the company and I began to pass the company. And as I reached the head of the company, here comes Major Davis. He had made a big circle and was coming down the road meeting the company again. Well fortunately, even though I was wringing wet with perspiration and breathing rather heavily, I stretched myself up to my 5 ft. 7 and ¼ inches and rendered a tremendous hand salute and he returned it in kind and rode on. So, I knew I had passed the test for that day at least.

Colonel Stokely, the regimental commander, was transferred to another organization and we were assigned a Colonel James A. Van Fleet as a regimental commander. Colonel James A. Van Fleet became a general officer, four stars general, later and has a tremendous military record. In the stories to follow, I will mention Colonel or General Van Fleet on several occasions. But in my mind, he's one of the greatest leaders that the U.S. has ever produced. After he joined the Regiment, and Colonel Van Fleet had assumed command of the Regiment and been there awhile and began to know the officers pretty well, we received orders one day that we were getting in a large number of recruits. So, Colonel Van Fleet, for some reason, selected me to be the recruit training officer for this large number of recruits that we were getting in. The day that these troops arrived, I met the train with my cadre of a few noncommissioned officers and I had a sergeant Eubanks from Charleston, South Carolina who was going to be my first sergeant. We met the train and I remind you that the 8th Infantry Regiment was a New York regiment. So, off the trains that day we got 500 individuals from New York City and Brooklyn. We proceeded to take them out to the Harmony Church area where the 8th Regiment was located and do processing of drawing individual clothing and equipment. When that was completed, the next day Sergeant Eubanks got all these individuals in a formation, and I was going to give them a little talk about how things were going to run in this organization while they were under my command. So, we had them lined up on a rather large field adjacent to the regimental area. They work in two ranks. While I was giving them my instructions of how this situation was going to develop and what they would be expected to do etc., I noticed lots of nudging of each other in ranks and whispering. So, I stopped my dissertation and called the first sergeant. I said, "first sergeant." Sergeant Eubanks moved out smartly, came up to me and rendered a smart salute and I returned it and said, "First sergeant, what in the hell is going on?" And without hesitation, he blushed and said, "Sir, I hate to tell you, but they don't understand a word you're saying." So, my only retort was, "Well dammit, I'll teach them how to fight if they will teach me how to speak their lingo." I'd tried to learn the lingo of the Brooklynite, but I was never able to emulate them or copy their accent. But I did have to change my dialect somewhat in order to be understood.

One day Harold Mowese and I got to talking. And he said that he had applied to join the Army Air Corps and had been accepted. And he began to talk to me about applying. So, the more we talked, the more interested I became, and finally decided that, sure enough, I would apply to transfer to the Army Air Corps. So, we went over to the airfield at Fort Benning, Ga., the name of it escapes me right now, and applied and submitted my application and stood a physical examination. We came on back to the 8th Regiment and it wasn't long thereafter, a couple days after I submitted my application, I received word that Colonel Van Fleet, the regimental commander, wanted to see me. So, I began to wonder what in the world I had done wrong that would generate interest by the regimental commander. So, I reported to Colonel Van Fleet and he said, "is it true that you have submitted an application to transfer to the Army Air Corps?" I said, "yes sir." And he proceeded to ask me a few questions. For example, he said, "have you ever been up in an airplane?" I said, "no sir." "How do you know you'll like it?" I said, "Sir, I don't know whether I'd like it or not." Well, such questions as this, I got the point rather early that he was trying to talk me out of letting my application be considered. So, after some further discussion, I decided to withdraw my application, which I did. Mowese did get his application approved and transferred to the Army Air Corps, later the Army Air Force.

After having given those recruits which had been assigned to the 8th Infantry Regiment about eight weeks of basic infantry training, they were then assigned to companies within the 8th Infantry Regiment, and I returned to F Company. By this time, a Captain Kerns had arrived and assumed command of F Company. So, I went back to a platoon leader within F Company instead of being company commander.

While still at Fort Benning, Ga., it was determined that the Fourth Infantry Division would become a Fourth Provisional Motorized Division. And as a result, we were issued many old trucks. Now how they were able to assemble all these old trucks, I don't know, but we did have sufficient trucks to move the entire division. Now, we had no experience factors, time/space factors, with reference to a motorized division. So, it was decided the Fourth Infantry Division would conduct a motor march, and if I remember correctly, to Panama City, Florida. During this march, one regiment would march as a coordinate convoy, in other words, you would have serials and a hundred yards between vehicles and really monitored very closely, a complete convoy. And one regiment would try the infiltration method. Now regarding the infiltration method, apparently someone came up with the idea that since we had so many people from New York City, for example, and large cities, obviously they've driven automobiles and trucks so they should be able to drive a truck along the highway. And they were given a strip map and told where to report and what time for the night that you could make more time by infiltrating using the infiltration method. Well, the Eight Regiment was selected to try this. And I tell you the truth, I've never seen such a show in my life, because many of these soldiers could drive automobiles and trucks, but this was freedom that they had not expected to enjoy. So, one would be riding down the highway, going a reasonable speed, 35-40-45 miles per hour and some truck would come pass by. The soldiers would take off their head gear and they'd be charging down the highway and after you had gone about 35 miles, we would see the truck pulled off to one side and the soldiers visiting a store or country store drinking pop. Well, to make a long story short, using that system, we had trucks scattered from Fort Benning, Georgia all the way to Panama City for about three days before we could corral them. During the second night on the road, we spent the night at Natchez, Mississippi and a large field had been designated as an assembly area for the regiment. Well, even though I painted a gloomy picture about the convoy and the infiltration method, many troops did get there to the designated assembly area and I must say, it was a phased basis as they started arriving about noon and they filled in the designated assembly area, coming in the late afternoon. It was no use to try to set up base camp until everyone arrived. We waited until it was late in the afternoon. It was a cloudy day and we were in a tremendous alfalfa field. Finally, it was time to set up tents. Now we had to set up the pup tents or two-man tents again in rows. The company street had to be surveyed in and every tent lined up perfectly. Well, when this procedure started, the rabbits in this alfalfa field began to get disturbed and would start running. You could see a group of soldiers trying to put up a pup tent in a given area, and all of a sudden tents would fall and troops would start running after rabbits, hollering at the top of their voices, "here," and they'd surge over this way, lose a rabbit and the rabbit would cut back through the assembly area and then another group would pick it up, "here," and run over other people's tent and just about the time you get going again, another rabbit would jump from another place and this crowd would surge this way. That went on for about an hour. Pretty soon, the commander had to get out there and direct that there would be no more rabbit chasing. Finally, we got the tents up and just about the time everyone had settled down, the biggest downpour of rain occurred that I think I have ever seen. This alfalfa field turned into a lake and I remember very well trying to sleep in this pup tent. And the rain was so heavy that the tent began to leak but not only that, the water began to come under it. Even though we had run drainage trenches around the tent, that didn't stop it. Pretty soon, the water was at least 6 inches deep in the tent and if you got up, your blanket would float out. Well this was a new experience to many young soldiers and two went berserk and started running down through the battalion area. Finally, somebody corralled them and turned them over to medics. But I was thinking that night how things like this can upset people to such a degree that it would just snap their minds. It was a rough one. It was a rough night.

Now later in the year, maybe it was the beginning of early 1941. The division was ordered to participate in the Louisiana maneuvers, which meant that we would motor down to Dry Prawn, Louisiana and participate in a very large maneuver. Upon arrival, I was designated to assist in the umpire headquarters. But prior to my going up to umpire headquarters, I was with the battalion and we moved in to a national forest there at Dry Prawn, Louisiana. And I remember very well the afternoon we pulled in to this particular area and began to try and set up a battalion bivouac area. By actual count, within the battalion area, we killed 36 rattlesnakes within an hour and 30 minutes. In addition, there were many coral snakes. But there's also a snake that looks just like a coral snake, but the colors are reversed. Well, many soldiers became quite upset because they thought that those snakes, that that looked like corral snakes, were coral snakes but we had to instruct everyone that this was not the case. But speaking of the rattlesnake, I remember the next day I was taking a patrol out to check the Battalion perimeter and it was early morning, the grass was wet with dew, and I had heard all my life that you should not be the third man in a column when marching through or walking through snake infested country. This particular morning, I was the fourth man. I really didn't think about that, until this particular incident that I'm about to tell about happened. We were walking along, and in those days, we wore these canvas leggings, and when they got wet, they would tighten up and, when we came across a log, the first soldier stepped over the log and nothing happened. The second soldier stepped over the log and nothing happened. The third soldier stepped over it and a rattlesnake hit his legging. Well fortunately, as I say the leggings were wet and it had tightened up and that snakes' fangs slid off of his legging. We naturally, we killed it. But I've often thought about that since that day. I try to avoid being the third man in a column when on a walk through a snake infested area. And the theory is that the first man alerts the snake, the second irritates him and the third, he's been irritated so much he'll strike. Whether this is true or not, I don't know but it's a pretty good theory.

As I said earlier, I left the battalion and detailed to work in the maneuver headquarters. And there, I was responsible for maintaining, assisting and maintaining a big map that showed the location of all organizations, down to battalion sized units that were participating as red and blue forces. There is where I got to see a newly promoted General Mark Clark, General McNair, General Lear, and all those famous general officers who were outstanding officers then but really became more famous later. And all of them really impressed me a great deal. General Eisenhower, all of them. But we did have our problems as you may understand. We had been training these soldiers to be aggressive at all times and now we were in a maneuver. And I think we were a little lax in cautioning our soldiers to be aggressive but to exercise some restraint, particularly during a maneuver, because you really are not fighting the enemy. That's the members of your own army that you'll be fighting. But don't get mixed up by a rifle butt or fist fight. Well, in that we apparently didn't do this to the degree required, we at maneuver headquarters were ceased with reports of fistfights and fighting each other with rifle butts. I recall one situation where two battalions became involved in a fight and the battalion commander was hit with a rifle butt by a soldier of the opposing force and it knocked him over in a creek and he fell on a log and it broker his back. Well, when cases like this occurred, we had to put out strict instructions. And then umpires were instructed to take disciplinary action if such fights occurred. Another thing that we learned during that maneuver is when one force captures vehicles of the opposing force, they are not suppose to take the keys out of the vehicle and leave them stranded in the pine woods, which happened on many occasions. In addition, we had quite a few horse calvary units and we had a tremendous problem such as a horse cavalry troop being captured by an opposing force. They would take the riders off of the horses and tie the horses to trees in the woods and just abandon them. Well now you know this is inhumane and any cavalryman knows the last thing you do is take care of that horse first. Well, maneuver headquarters was jumping through the hoop, so to speak, trying to correct these types of deficiencies. And later, I was instrumental in helping to write an umpire's manual which was disseminated throughout the army as to how soldiers should perform, what you should do when a vehicle is captured and what you should not do. Well, the Louisiana maneuvers was an extremely fine teaching vehicle. We all learned a great deal during those maneuvers that stood us in good stead. For example, the old peacetime army, they used to travel first class, so to speak, such as battalion commander. He had a small wool tent and a cot was taken along for him and a one-hole latrine was taken and a lot of impedimental creature comfort items. Well, I heard General McNair blast a couple of general officers who commanded a couple divisions, fortunately it wasn't General Barton. He says that, "by God, you brought everything to include the kitchen sink and you better get rid of it immediately or you will be relieved." So, he meant business, and it was a good test. It was a good shake down crew, so to speak. And with reference to the Fourth Motorized

Division, it gave us an opportunity, members of the division, it gave us an opportunity to shake down and then we got a real feel of how a motorized organization would operate. For example, the division would be on one flank, late in the afternoon, and then they would move all night and attack the opposing forces on the opposite flank the next night. So those people who thought you could ride all the time, and therefore didn't have to walk so they joined a motorized division. That was well and good, but you never got any sleep and you were always in the attack. In addition, we found that the infiltration method of moving troops by a vehicle was impractical. And I don't believe that I've ever seen more then one short paragraph devoted to that type movement in any field manual.

Earlier I stated that the division commander was major General Raymond O. Barton. That is wrong. Major General Fredendall was still the division commander when we were at Fort Benning. General Barton became the division commander later. General Fredendall, as I mentioned earlier, he was a man about 5'-8" tall. So, he was a little man compared to the famous General Patton, who was commander of the Second Armored Division stationed at Sand Hill. There was a great deal of professional rivalry between General Fredendall and General Patton when we were stationed out in the Harmony Church area. At the time, General Fredendall, being the senior was Commanding General of the Fourth Infantry Division, also post commander of the main post at Fort Benning. And one day, a military policeman picked up General Patton for speeding. Now General Fredendall called General Patton in on the carpet and apparently chewed him out pretty good. Well General Patton didn't forget this. So, one day, General Fredendall was called away to Washington on some professional business, so that left General Patton the senior commander of the Second Armored Division and acting post commander at Fort Benning. This particular morning, I was going into the main post to pick up the pay for the troops. As I got to the military police post, on First Division Road, as I entered the main post, there was no MP on duty. I stopped, got out and checked around the area of the MP post and no one was there so I proceeded on down to the finance center and got my pay and stopped by the officer's club for a cool drink of some kind and pretty soon I heard a tremendous rumbling going on, and I couldn't imagine what all this noise was. It sounded like tanks. And incidentally, General Fredendall had told General Patton that he did not want any tanks running on the streets or roads of the main post of Fort Benning. Well, all this rumbling, it sounded to me like tanks and I wondered what in the world was going on. Pretty soon, I saw a complete combat command of tanks coming down First Division Road on the main post. Pretty soon, a tank cut out of the column, the leading tank cut out of the column and came up in the parking lot of the officer's club at Fort Benning. In those days, there was no hard stand around the club, just dirt. And the tank spun around and out stepped General Patton with his two-pearl handled pistol. He surveyed the situation. The combat command continued to roll down the main post and after they toured the main post, they took off back to Sand Hill. Well, what was happening was General Patton had relieved all the members of the military police on duty on the main post and cranked up a combat command and toured it all through the main post of Fort Benning just to prove a point to General Fredendall that while he was in command, that he, General Patton, was in command, and he could do what he damned please.

Earlier I mentioned the rivalry that existed between organizations stationed at Fort Benning, Ga., and especially the professional rivalry between the Fourth Infantry Division and the Second Armored Division plus the personal rivalry between Major General Fredendall, the Commanding General of the Fourth Infantry Division and Major General George Patton, the Commanding General of the Second Armored Division. I'll never forget, once we had a maneuver which pitted the Second Armored Division against the Fourth Infantry Division on the reservation and surrounding area of Fort Benning, Ga. During that maneuver, the Second Armored Division really defeated the Fourth Infantry Division. There was no question about it. The Second Armored did defeat the Fourth Infantry Division. So, it was determined that there would be a large critique after the exercise terminated. All officers and senior noncommissioned officers of both divisions were assembled at the big drop zone, airborne drop zone, on Hourglass Road. This particular morning, General Patton got on the speaker's stand and everyone expected a fiery speech, in a help nation and brimstone-type presentation. And to our utter amazement, General Patton's presentation was very mild because his division had won the exercise and apparently his spirits were very high. Well, when he finally sat down after complimenting everyone, particularly the members of the Second Armored Division, the roster was turned over to General Fredendall. When General Fredendall jumped up to the microphone, his first words were, "let's stop pissing up and down each other's back. This maneuver stunk." And then he began to tell why it did stink. Well, he outdid General Patton by far. And it was one of the most profane presentations I've ever heard. But this just illustrated the rivalry between these two individuals. And after that experience, I predicted that if these two commanders ever got to a combat theater, and they could not find enough enemy to fight, and keep them both busy, that they would fight each other. And so, it happened later during World War Two, both General Fredendall and General Patton were in Afrika, North Afrika, and they engaged in some type of confrontation. As a result, General Patton won out. General Fredendall was shipped back to the United States.

While stationed at Fort Benning, Ga., I was also dating my elementary school and high school sweetheart, one by the name of Eulena Evans Myers who lived at Haygood, South Carolina. I was getting rather serious about marriage. So, I proposed to my future wife, Een Mabry, and we were married in Haygood, South Carolina on October 16, 1941. After being married, I took my young bride back to Columbus, Ga. And rented a one room abode from a lady living in Columbus, Ga. The one room was sufficient at that time because, due to the stress of training, both day and night, I would very seldom get home for any extended period. But I shall never forget, and I'm sure Een won't forget the evening of December 7th, 1941. And you will remember this date as Pearl Harbor Day. I had come home that evening and Een and I decided to go see a movie in Columbus. While sitting in the movie theater, the announcement was made for all military personnel to report immediately to their respective unit and organization. Well, Een and I immediately left. And I dashed her back to our one room castle and I took off for Fort Benning. Having turned on the radio, we found out that Pearl Harbor had been attacked by the Japanese. Now I must admit here that I really didn't know where Pearl Harbor was. But anyway, we knew that the United States property, possession had been attacked by the Japanese. Therefore, the United States would probably be at war with the Japanese the following day.

Upon reaching Company F out at Harmony Church, the company, battalion, regiment and the entire division was a beehive of activity. To make a long story short, we loaded ammunition all night long, not only in trucks, but also in machine-gun belts, we broke down the ammunition for each soldier and stood by to receive further orders. Some orders were issued and small detachments of men were dispatched to strategic railroad crossings, or trestles, and major highway intersections and posted as guards. I assumed that someone at the highest level was concerned about possible sabotage. But this experience really shook us because it was quite obvious that the United States would not only become involved in a major conflict in Europe but also in the Pacific.

About this time, it was announced that the Fourth Infantry Division, Fourth Provisional Motorized Division, would be moved from Fort Benning, Ga. to a new camp that was being constructed to accommodate the Fourth Motorized Division and that camp was Camp Gordon at Augusta, Ga. We had begun to receive a few half trucks, which the division would be equipped with completely once we arrived at Camp Gordon, Ga. We moved from Fort Benning to Camp Gordon, Augusta, Ga. and began to settle in this new camp. Fortunately, barracks had been built for personnel purposes and administrative purposes. In addition, large motor pools had been constructed with a lot of hardstand (paved area) so that we could park our half tracks and work on them properly. Each squad in the division had a half track, so you could imagine the number of vehicles that even a company had. And you multiply that be the number of companies in a battalion and on up through Division, I just don't remember the total number of vehicles that the Fourth Motorized Division had, but a tremendous amount of our time was spent in maintaining these vehicles properly. That did not lessen the requirement as training as infantry soldiers, because we looked upon the vehicles and the half-tracks as a means of transportation rather than a fighting vehicle. So, we walked a lot and we trained a lot as straight infantrymen and then got in the vehicles as a means of transportation from Point A to Point B rather than a fighting vehicle like a tank.

There was a new Battalion commander of the Second Battalion, 8th Regiment, and his name was something like Lieutenant Colonel Woodrow. That's not his name, but it's similar to that. And he was a good man but he tended to drink excessively on occasions. I can remember one day I was out on the rifle range and the battalion commander and I had been talking when the regimental commander, Colonel James a. Van Fleet, a teetotaler, approached us and began to talk about the firing that was ongoing on the range and finally, this battalion commander left to do something. And Colonel Van Fleet turned to me and said, "George, have you been drinking?"

And I said, "Sir, you know I have not been drinking. I don't drink." And then he said, "has the battalion commander been drinking?" I said, "Sir, I don't know but if I did, I would not tell you." And he looked at me and said, "you're right. Forget I asked the question." But later, Colonel Van Fleet got rid of this battalion commander because he, Colonel Van Fleet, found that this battalion commander was drinking at night rather excessively and the smell of alcoholic beverage was on his breath during duty hours. So, Colonel Van Fleet got rid of him. We then acquired a battalion commander by the name of Carlton O. McNeeley, from Columbus, Ga. Now Lieutenant Colonel Carlton O. McNeeley turned out to be a tremendous individual. He was a leader of the First War, charming personality, very sensitive but could be tough and was tough when it was required. On the other hand, he respected the individuals and would fight for the rights of his soldiers.

Now General Marshall was then the chief of the army, maybe chief of staff of the whole War Department, and he would be visiting Camp Gordon. We had received word that General Marshall would visit the 8th Infantry Regiment. Colonel Van Fleet had instructed Colonel McNeeley to be at regimental headquarters because Colonel Van Fleet wanted General Marshall to visit the Second Battalion of the 8th Regiment. Colonel McNeeley took me along with him to regimental headquarters to meet the visiting party. We arrived at the appointed time and soon, General Barton, escorting General Marshall arrived at regimental headquarters. Colonel Van Fleet ran out and reported to General Marshall and began to introduce the people standing around, like Colonel McNeeley and myself. And as soon as the introduction had been completed, General Marshall turned to Colonel Van Fleetand said, "Van, why are you still a colonel?" Colonel Van Fleet says, "Sir, I don't know. What do you mean?" And General Marshall turned to General Barton, the division commander, and said, "Tubby, Van is still a colonel? Haven't you recommended him for promotion? General Barton said, "General Marshall, I have recommended Van on three separate occasions, but every time I recommend him for a promotion, I get the word back it's been disapproved." And General Marshall stood there a moment and says, "my gracious alive! I am the cause of that. Let me tell you what happened. I had you mixed up with that sot by the name of Van Vleet." Now Van Vleet, as I remember, was a signal officer and was a good officer but he apparently did drink too much to suit General Marshall. General Marshall then said, "your name has come across my desk in the way of recommendation for promotion, and every time I see it, I think of Van Vleet and I tear it up and throw it in the trash basket under the assumption that we do not want a drunken sot as a general officer in our army." And General Barton said, "well I wondered. I thought there was something peculiar because Van here is doing an outstanding job," etc. And General Marshall said a few other things and I walked away but I heard this much. They continued to discuss it. But later I learned General Marshall said that when he went back to Washington, that he would see that Van Fleet was promoted immediately. Then General Barton entered the discussion and said, "well, General Marshall, you know what's in store for the Fourth Division. And Van has been here as regimental commander and I would like to keep him as regimental commander until we get into combat." And later, I heard that this was agreed to. And it must be true because Colonel Van Fleet stayed as regimental commander until after we landed in Normandy on D-day and was assured that we were ashore to stay. And then, he was transferred and immediately promoted.

Now, we were finally told one day that we would have a mounted review. That meant that every vehicle of the Fourth Infantry Division would be lined up on the tremendously large parade ground at Camp Gordon, Augusta, Ga. And at the appropriate time, after the foot troops had marched in review, the entire motorized elements of the Fourth Division would pass in review. A General McNair would be the reviewing officer. We assembled that morning and the array of vehicles stretched out over that field was something to behold. We started the parade, the review about 9:00, as I recall. The foot troops marched past and then the vehicles began to move. And there were at least four vehicles abreast. And this stream of vehicles started coming by while General McNair and the other reviewing officers were on the reviewing stand. I marched back to the company with the foot elements of F Company and did some work. And then I walked back down to the parade field and the vehicles were still passing in review. Well they must have passed in review for at least four and a half if not five hours. When the last vehicle came by, there was no grass on the parade field. It looked like a dust bowl. Gas cans and impediments of all kinds littered the entire parade field. Someone told me that General McNair had made the comment that it would be impossible to assemble enough shipping to ship the Fourth Infantry Division overseas. Well, based on that and other things, I felt that the Fourth Motorized Division was not to exist very much longer.

Also, when we were still stationed at Fort Benning, the Carolina maneuvers transpired. During these maneuvers, I would move around at night on foot within the bivouac area and listen to conversations of soldiers. I learned a great deal about how soldiers felt about noncommissioned officers and officers in the company. Now I pause here to remind anyone listening that this is a good practice. But never divulge to anyone what you say or what is said by individuals to whom you are listening. On occasion, you will hear uncomplimentary remarks about other people and specifically about yourself. It would be a tragic mistake, however, to jump out of the bushes and grab the individual who was making the comment and chastise him. Well, some of the things I learned was that during conversations between soldiers, if you heard them make a comment about one of the noncommissioned officers or soldiers to the effect that, "yeh, he is a good guy," then you better catalog that in your mind and take a look at that noncommissioned officer or officer because that's really not a complimentary term. There's something wrong. Either he's too lenient or something is being done that this soldier knows should not be done and that officer or noncommissioned officer is not making appropriate corrections. On the other hand, if you hear the expression, "well, he's tough, but he's a good man," now that's a compliment indeed, because in that case the individual about whom they are talking is tough but he's a good man. They would follow him anywhere, because he's practicing the proper procedures of leadership. Now there are a lot of famous men and other less famous who had nicknames. For example, Black Jack Pershing, and as I mentioned, Bull Holland and the Iron Duke Duffner. Well during these maneuvers, I learned my nickname, and it was the *mean little one*. Now on occasion, I did hear comments that indicated that I was fair, but tough. So, the nickname *the mean little one* was normally used as *little one*. But it was just understood that the word "mean" should precede the nickname "little one."

During the summer of 1942, the division was alerted for overseas movement. This was the first of several false alarms the division experienced because on Christmas Day of December '42, the division was again alerted for overseas movement. We packed, crated and marked all equipment and all personnel underwent physical examinations in preparation for the movement. However, this alert did not materialize so we began to gradually uncrate material and commence training more vigorously than ever. I was told later that the division was destined to join the allied forces in North

Afrika, but sufficient shipping could not be assembled to transport the large number of half tracks and other vehicles with which we were equipped. To tell you the truth, I really didn't want to go into combat with those half-tracks, because I named them the Purple Heart wagons. The reason I called them this was due to the large number of bolts, taps and rivets that held them together. I could just imagine what would happen when an armored piercing round were to hit one of the half-tracks. Taps, bolts, and rivets I'm sure would have sprayed the area like shotgun pellets. In addition, the half-track had no overhead cover as protection against artillery and mortar fire. I might pause here and inject that the newly assembled Fourth Division had begun training together since August 1940. However, the division was called upon on several occasions to provide large numbers of enlisted men, noncommissioned officers and officers to constitute cadres for new divisions and other smaller organizations which were being organized during this mass expansion of the army and armed forces. Somehow, I along with several other old-timers, so to speak, survived these drawdowns and remained with the Fourth. Some other officers who escaped the cadre drawdown and who played prominent roles in combat later were Lieutenant James W. "Chick" Haley, Marcus Long de Powell, Walter Todd, Bill McCleary, Bob Witherington, Jack Meyer, Omar Bates, Fred Collins, and a few others.

In April 1943, the division was ordered to move to Fort Dix, New Jersey. And in August '43, the Fourth Motorized Division, after reaching Fort Dix, was redesignated as the Fourth Infantry Division. So, we turned in all those Purple Heart wagons and began to concentrate on straight infantry tactics again. Soon after arrival at Fort Dix, a rather unique thing happened. There was a labor shortage in the area because so many men had been drafted for the armed forces. In view of this, a rather large segment of the division was turned out to help harvest the tomato crop in New Jersey. This project went very well. But noncommissioned officers who were supervising the detail of picking tomatoes had to, on many occasions, halt tomato throwing fights which developed between the soldiers.

To give you an idea of how mobile a second lieutenant or a lieutenant had to be, I was a first lieutenant at that time, and his wife were, when we got to Fort Dix, the only thing we could find in the way of housing was a room in a private home in Brown's Mill, New Jersey. Capt. And Mrs. Al Yarborough also had a room there. Now this was a rather cramped quarters, so we heard about a house that was available for rent in Bay Shore, New Jersey, for about one month in duration. So, the four of us decided to rent that house for the short period that it would be available. Accordingly, we moved to Bay Shore and stayed there for about a month. Now we had to turn the house over, so Een and I moved to an apartment in New Egypt. And later, we moved to Mount Holly and that was the last place we stayed prior to being transferred to another location. So, we moved five times in five months. The apartment we had in New Egypt was really a dilly. Apparently, a store owner on Main Street of New Egypt went out of business, so he converted the store into a two-apartment house. Our apartment was on the ground floor. The small living room occupied the space immediately behind the large glass storefront on which was still painted advertisements of the store. Now many local farmers had been accustomed to shopping in this particular store, so we were disturbed at night on many occasions by local farmers rattling the door and demanding to be admitted to purchase items. This occurred especially on Saturday nights. I believe that possibly after the store closed, it might have been turned into a café or cafeteria for a short period of time.

I had been promoted to first lieutenant in November 1941 and to captain in August '42 and was now commanding Headquarters Company of the Second Battalion, 8th Regiment. Even though I was a company commander, I was still responsible for coaching the regimental baseball team during the season and the boxing team during its respective season. In addition, the regimental commander, Colonel James A. Van Fleet, put the finger on me to teach every newly assigned second lieutenant, first lieutenant and captain how to render the hand salute properly and how to give voice commands and instruct them in the fine techniques of close order drill. This training was conducted in a large field adjacent to regimental headquarters where Colonel Van Fleet could monitor the progress of my students. The turning lasted for about seven days. Initially, I would get these officers and instruct them on how to give voice commands, for example. Having done that, I would separate them, say fifty yards apart initially, and have each one give voice commands and then increase the distances until they were 200 to 250 yards apart. On many occasions, Colonel Van Fleet would come by to see me and pointed out officers who had weak command voices and jot down their names. I soon learned that those who had weak command voices and showed little improvement would have a difficult time becoming company commanders in the Eight Regiment, because soldiers respect and respond quickly, much more quickly to those leaders who have clear command voices in addition, of course, to other qualifications. For example, I would instruct officers that, in order to render commands properly, the command must come from the diaphragm. And the preparatory command would have to be lengthened somewhat so that one would be sure that every man understood what was coming. Then, the command of execution had to be very sharp and crisp. For example, and I'll lower my voice rather than do it in a normal manner, for example, right face. The command should be and have the proper tempo and crispness such as RI-I-I-I-IGHT... FACE. Now if you know it, "right" is rather long compared to the command of execution. But this timing and tempo gives the soldiers a second or two to be sure he understands what you want done. The command of execution should be very sharp, so that every man does it with precision.

My baseball team won the championship while at Fort Dix. And I had an excellent team and a very superior pitcher by the name of Speck. My boxing team didn't fare as well in the preliminary fights. Now I remember after one preliminary fight in the early stages of my training the boxing team, I had noted that many of my young fighters failed to show the proper degree of aggressiveness during their fights. Before I could do anything about that, in fact, the next morning after the preliminary bouts were held, I received a call to report to Colonel Van Fleet. So, I went into his office. He asked me to have a seat and he began to talk about the preliminary bouts that he had attended the night before. And he began to talk about the lack of aggressiveness on the part of a couple of my young fighters. And it was obvious to him and me that one fighter in particular had a great deal of potential but it appeared that he was not sure of himself. So, while we were discussing this, finally Colonel Van Fleet said, "get up and let me show you what you need to train him to do." Now his back was turned to a private entrance into his office from the outside of the building. The wooden door was open and the screen door was shut. Colonel Van Fleet was saying, "now you've got to get that left arm out a little further and he's got to move in with that left hand and shoot a left and follow it right up with a right hand and get the one-two punch." And finally, he said, "stand over here and let me show you what I'm talking about." So, I got up and was standing where I could see the door. And just as I began to raise my arms to take the boxing stance so Colonel Van Fleet could illustrate his point, I noted someone approaching the door. And all of a sudden it dawned on me that it was General Barton, the division commander. Well I froze. General Barton, seeing what was going on, stood on the steps and did not come in. Well about this time, Colonel Van Fleet said, "put up your dukes, George. Put up your dukes." So, I was about to take the boxing stance again and I became flustered, didn't know what to do so I merely half-pointed to the door behind Colonel Van Fleet. He didn't catch what I was doing. And finally, in a weak voice I said, "Sir, General Barton." Well, Colonel Van Fleet turned around immediately and both of us stood at attention. And Colonel Van Fleet reported to General Barton and General Barton walked in, stood there looking at Colonel Van Fleet and in a very serious voice said, "well, I've been wondering, Colonel Van Fleet, how you've been able to maintain such good discipline in the Eight Regiment. I now see how you do it. You beat up on small second lieutenants and captains as an example to other members of the division, eh?" Well this flustered Colonel Van Fleet very much because he, Colonel Van Fleet, played football at the academy (was an outstanding tackle) and was over 6 ft. tall and hear me, a little captain, 5 ft 7 and ¼ inches and Colonel Van Fleet began to flip his arms around and began to apologize. And General Barton apparently was enjoying this immensely. So, he strung Colonel Van Fleet around a little bit and laughingly spoke to me and said he understood what was going and predicted that I would probably win the championship again this year with my team. So, I finally requested to be excused and permission was granted, so I beat a hasty retreat out of Colonel Van Fleet's office.

In early September 1943, the division received orders to head south again. Our destination was Camp Gordon Johnston at Carol Bell, Florida, on the shores of the Gulf of Mexico where the division would undergo extensive amphibious training in anticipation of the invasion of Europe. By this time, I saw without hesitation that the Fourth Division was one of the best trained divisions in the United States Army. Not only had we been trained as an infantry division but also as a motorized division. We had fired every weapon the U.S. Army had in its arsenal. And now we were going to receive amphibious training. Upon arrival at Camp Gordon Johnston, it must have been obvious to all members of the division that training would be the order of both day and night because the closest town was Tallahassee, some 50 miles away. And we were really in the boondocks. The troop housing consisted of long, narrow tarpaper shacks. And the deep Florida sand constituted the floors thereof. There were no recreational facilities whatsoever for the troops. So, during the little free time available for the soldiers, many of them would go out in the swamps and catch small alligators and stake them out as pets in a small creek that ran through the battalion area. The lack of recreational facilities was so critical it was finally decided to legalize gambling with cards and dice tables in the company areas provided these games were supervised by officers and noncommissioned officers. This was done and so due to the close supervision exercised, we had no unpleasant incidents that I can recall. After the games closed at night, many soldier's picked up a considerable amount of loose change by sifting the Florida sand around the game tables. This was also done in the barracks area because soldiers taking off their trousers, etc., would lose change. And by sifting the sand, it became rather profitable to many soldiers.

While stationed at Camp Gordon Johnston, my headquarters placed additional emphasis on the requirement for all combat-type units to make one 25-mile march once each month. Now this was quite a chore in Florida, because it was not only hot but the sand was deep. But that requirement was required for the Fourth Infantry Division. Accordingly, once each month the mess personnel of the company mess hall would preposition large cans of soup, like bouillon soup, at a specific location along the route which the units would take during their 25-mile hike which they needed to complete within eight hours. So, dressed in combat uniforms and wearing a light pack, we would strike out and jog for a considerable distance and then walk a bit and then jog. About noontime, we would reach the location where the bullion-type soup was stationed. So one would, while jogging, take out the canteen out of the canteen cover, and remove the canteen cup from the cover in which the canteen nestled, and put the canteen back in the canteen cover and hold the aluminum cup and as you jogged by these cans of soup, you would get a half/three-quarters cup of soup and then drink it while continuing to march and jog. Now many men suffered blisters and shin splints and all kinds of ailments, but many of the officers would, in order to prove how tough, they were, we would make the march and then get up a softball game in a little vacant lot in Florida sand and play.

One day, Colonel Van Fleet and the regimental assistant, a Lieutenant Ross, and a couple of other people went out on a reconnaissance to find

29

some terrain that Colonel Van Fleet wanted to use to give all our soldiers additional experience. So, they went through a considerable amount of jungle and found a creek. On one side of the creek there was quite a bit of mud on the bank. On the opposite side of the creek, the current was rather swift and it was a fairly steep bank. So, Colonel Van Fleet and these officers, wearing their light pack and combat equipment, swam across the creek, turned round and swam back. As they reached the near bank again, as I say, it was rather muddy and boggy, just as Lieutenant Ross reached that portion, he disappeared. And the other members in the group waited a second or two and he didn't appear again. So, Colonel Van Fleet and the other members of the party began diving to try to locate Lieutenant Ross. Their valiant efforts proved unsuccessful, for the word was brought back to the regiment. Then additional personnel went out and attempted to find Lieutenant Ross' body. Eventually, it was located lodged up against some roots on the further side of the creek where the current was swift. Apparently, he had some cramps or something, but he was a good swimmer. Unfortunately, the current took him out into the stream and washed him up under the bank where the current had eaten away the under portions of the bank. Well, this was a tragedy. And naturally, Colonel Van Fleet was as upset as anyone else. But he, recognizing that many of us would probably die when we got into combat, directed that every man in that regiment would swim that creek at the same location where Lieutenant Ross drowned. The only additional safety feature that was provided was a rope strung across the creek so that if anyone got into difficulty, he might float down and catch hold of the rope and then propel himself across the dark water creek which had a fairly swift current. And this was done. Every man in the regiment, at least I know every man in the Second Battalion, went across that creek. And I admired Colonel Van Fleets directive in this regard, because to be sure, we would suffer other casualties later.

By this time, I had become S-3 of the Second Battalion. Now the S-3 means operation training officer of the battalion. The amphibious training, we underwent at Camp Gordon Johnston was most valuable and it was most demanding. As the S-3, it was my duty to fill out what we call boat loading team tables. By that I mean that we would have to assume we were aboard a ship. And in order to get from ship to shore, individuals and equipment, vehicles of all kinds would have to be loaded from the ship into smaller craft and then taken ashore. Well, it was the S-3's duty to work up these boat loading tables to ensure that the proper type of vehicle went into the appropriate boat and that the proper personnel went in each boat. And you had to divide these boats into waves, such as the first wave was assault troops, and the second wave, and the third wave and finally the reserve company of the battalion, and so forth. Well this was constantly changing because, for example, constant changes to made to the number of LCVP's (landing craft carrying vehicle/personnel). Now the landing (craft) vehicle/personnel was a rather small boat. It had a ramp in front and soldiers and say, a few combat vehicles like a quarter ton jeep. The LCM, the landing craft mechanized, would take a tank and maybe one or two jeeps, plus some personnel. Well, you had to know the dimension of these amphibious transport vehicles and exactly how many men and how much equipment and how many vehicles could be fitted into them. So, this was invaluable experience to me, because later, when we were preparing for the invasion of France, we made out many, many combinations of boat loading tables to satisfy any eventuality because we did not know how many LCVP's, LCM's and so forth we'd have available.

It was announced that the division would culminate its training with a large-scale division amphibious exercise in the Gulf of Mexico. In preparation for this exercise, it was determined that a lieutenant and a sergeant from the Third Battalion would make a reconnaissance of the beach on which we were going to land in order to get intelligence about the beach, etc. under the assumption that we may be called upon to do a similar thing when we participated in the actual invasion of Europe. Well, this lieutenant and sergeant were taken out in an LCVP, out into the gulf and turned around and headed back toward the beach. Then they were unloaded from the LCVP into a rubber raft. It had a couple of paddles. Unfortunately, the wind got up and began to blow out to sea. Well, this lieutenant and sergeant began to paddle and I assumed that they thought they were making headway coming back to the beach when probably, the wind was taking them out plus the tide was taking them further out. And being pitch black dark, they could not be sure that they were making progress toward land. Well anyway, the next day they were reported missing because they had not come back and reported their findings pertaining to the beach and information about enemy installations. So, a limited search was made and they were not found. So then aircraft, air/sea rescue aircraft was dispatched and the entire division was turned out to search the shoreline. Not to the best of my knowledge, no trace of these two individuals nor their rubber boat or any of the equipment was ever located. So again, we did have an experience regarding another tragedy in the line of the duty.

About two weeks after that, the large-scale amphibious exercise for the entire division was set into motion. And everything went very well regarding loading the small craft. And we assume again that we were onboard a ship and late in the afternoon, the landing craft took out to sea. And after they got into their respective rendezvous areas, an unexpected storm came up. Now we were supposed to turn and land on the beaches at daylight the following morning. But with this storm, when the storm hit us, it scattered notes all over the Gulf of Mexico. And I recall very vividly what happened to my particular boat. We were touring around in the gulf and thought we were at a reasonable distance from the beach, but no other boats were near us. I became concerned and talked to the coxswain about it and finally he admitted that he didn't know where in the world he was. Naturally, under black out conditions, no lights, anything, so we began to tour around and hoping for daylight. It began to rain and it was a most uncomfortable situation. The waves were extremely high. So finally, about 3 o'clock in the morning, we happened to come upon another boat. So, we began to travel together. And it was an LCM. And I had been riding in the LCVP. Well, the fuel on the LCVP was just about to run out and the engine wasn't functioning properly. And about 45 minutes later, the LCVP conked out. So, I, being the S-3, thought I better transfer to the LCM and at least make it to the beach the next morning so I could help straighten out any confusion that might exist as a result of the storm mixing up waves and the landing group. So, I did. Well, we continued to tour around in the pitch-black dark on this LCM and about 4:30 in the morning, we heard many voices calling, "Help! Help!" So, we went in that direction and found about 25 men floating around in the Gulf of Mexico. Of course, they had their Mae West life jackets and they were hollering, "Help!" Apparently, their boat had overturned and they were just floating up and down on these tremendous waves. You would try to reach down and grab one of them and a wave would come and he would go above the boat and the next second, he would be down in the trough of a wave that looked like 50 feet below us.

It was quite a chore trying to rescue these men who were floating around in the gulf. Fortunately, some other boats were close by, which we didn't know at the time, and they converged and we were able to save these individuals. Well, this was not the only case. This was happening all throughout the division as it floated and meandered around in the gulf. Just prior to daylight, it became obvious to me, when the sun began to come up, that we were way off course. In fact, I estimated that we were off at least 20 to 25 miles out into the Gulf of Mexico. So, we took a dead reckoning course and headed for the beach. And I was quite disturbed because I knew it was impossible for us to make the landing on time, which had been set for, as I recall, about 6:30. But anyway, we took off and we passed other boats. Some of them were disabled. Others would call out and ask, "What company are your from?" And it was just confusion throughout the entire area. Well, to make a long story short, when the LCM I was riding on hit the beach, it was about 9:30 or 10 o'clock in the morning. We jumped out of the LCM and ran across the beaches, as we'd been taught to do, and we got beyond the beach line and I stopped and looked around and I didn't see another soul, no evidence that anybody had landed previously. Finally, I went down the beach and found one artillery gun, which was part of the 29th Field Artillery Battalion, and that was about all. The rest of the division was still floating around out in the Gulf of Mexico. Well, luckily it became rather obvious that maybe we really had a potential disaster on our hands. Aircraft, air/sea rescue aircraft were flying. And some troops that had been left back in the barracks had been mobilized like cooks, bakers and so forth and motorized vehicles were running up and down the beaches hoping to find landing craft and personnel who might have made it to shore.

Well, believe it or not, we didn't lose a man in the entire division from that fiasco. However, we did lose a tremendous amount of equipment. For example, one LCM just flipped over completely and lost two tanks. And some men were trapped under the LCM when it turned over. But fortunately, they had presence of mine to dive down and swim underwater and come up on the outside of this upturned craft. And come to think of it, we had taken extensive training and swimming while we were in Florida. For example, every man had to be able to swim. In addition, we went through an exercise where oil was poured over the water and set on fire. And we would dive in, swim underwater, come up through the burning oil and push it back by pushing water with the hand until you got a circle large enough to where you could breathe. Having done that and gotten the lungs full of fresh air, you would dive back down and swim out from under this burning oil and back to the bank and just demonstrate your proficiency to swim and also save one's self in the event of an emergency, like a shipwreck and burning oil is all over the water. So, this may have had some effect on the soldiers. And they kept calm during these emergencies that we were faced with as a result of the storm that really played havoc with the division amphibious exercise. But even with that, we learned a lot.

England

After undergoing extensive and profitable amphibious training at Camp Gordon Johnston, Florida, the division received orders to move to Fort Jackson at Columbia, South Carolina, and commence processing for overseas movement. Accordingly, the division arrived at Fort Jackson, South Carolina in December 1943 and began packing and crating all organizational equipment. Our stay at Fort Jackson was relatively short in duration. The division was then ordered to Camp Kilman, New Jersey in January 1944 for shipment overseas. The Second Battalion, plus other separate elements of the 8th Infantry Regiment, such as service company personnel, loaded aboard a ship named the Franconia. I believe it was an old French ship and many of the ship's crew were British. When we set sail from New York on January 24, 1944, it was soon learned that our ships would be one of a large group of ships that would be convoyed to England. In view of this, the speed of the convoy would be governed by the slowest ship within the convoy. Even though we had several Navy destroyers and submarines protecting our convoy, we had many anxious moments. On several occasions, the convoy was alerted to enemy submarines in the area and many depth charges were dropped by the destroyer escort. We ran into very rough weather on several occasions. This, combined with the British practice of serving kippid herring for breakfast fostered soldiers to become seasick. Additionally, as it is always the case among a group of men, the hardy souls did all they could to cause the weaker ones to get seasick. For example, conversations often turned to how wonderful it would be to have some nice greasy pork chops for lunch or for a snack. One of our doctors became seasick while the ship was tied to the pier in New York. And he never got out of the sick bay until we reached England. Conditions on board the Franconia were very crowded and the ship creaked, groaned and shuddered a great deal. But we made the crossing of the Atlantic in about 14 days and landed safely at the port of Liverpool, England.

Having debarked from the Franconia, members of the Second Battalion, 8th Infantry were transferred to the small seacoast resort village of Seaton, England, where we tried to settle down for additional training and waiting. The people of Seaton were very hospitable and we got along very well with them. The battalion executive officer and I lived in eight small summer-type cottage right on the edge of the English Channel. Before we arrived, a German plane had come over and strafed our particular cottage and left some bullet holes in windows and in the living room we had. On many occasions, the executive officer, my roommate, would escort visitors to the battalion through our little cottage and show them where the Germans strafed this little house. I didn't think too much about that at the time, because the executive officer had been a mentioned All-American football player and he was always talking about how, when he got into combat, he would tear these Nazis limb from limb. But more about that later. Other occasions, German bombers and fighters, while returning from raids on London and other areas on the interior of England, would drop a few bombs and strafe us on occasions on their way back across the channel. Now what they were doing were just jettisoning their bombs and having a little fun strafing us on their way back to their homeland, and most of them were stationed in France, I'm sure.

The people of Seaton could never get over how quietly the American troops marched. On many occasions, early in the morning we would be marching through Seaton and other little villages and people, as a custom in England, would throw open their windows, hang their bedding out of the window and be startled by all these troops that were moving through the village because they were accustomed to the British soldiers who wear the hobnail shoes and sang a lot. And some of the Britishers in Seaton and other areas began to question, maybe, the capabilities of the American soldier because it was such a contrast between the British hobnail shoes and the kind of swagger and their singing at all times whereas the Americans, we just walked through, no noise whatsoever. But it wasn't long before they realized that the American soldier was serious when it came to accomplishing a mission.

A little story about something that happened in Seaton one day: one Sunday afternoon, I was down around a little creek that ran through Seaton, England, and behind some bushes and I was looking at the swans swimming around on the creek. And there were a couple of soldiers sitting on a bridge watching the swans too. They didn't see me. And a Britisher came walking down the road and he approached the bridge. One of the soldiers said, "Hey there." The Britisher spoke to them and one of the soldiers asked, "What kind of birds are those swimming around out there?" And the Britisher said, "Those are swans." And one of the soldiers said, "Are they good to eat?" The Britisher said, "Oh yes, they're delicious, but they're reserved for the King and Queen of England." And the Britisher passed on. One soldier turned to the other and said, Man, if they're good enough for the King and Queen, well let's knock one of them off and roast and eat him." Well I thought I better step in on this. So, I walked up out of the bushes and talked to the soldiers and I said, "Soldiers, that Britisher said those swans were reserved for the King and Queen. What he meant is that they are a protected bird. And I heard you say something about knocking one of them off. Well, I'll tell you, if you knock one off, you'll create an international incident. And you better believe if I were to inform Colonel McNeeley about who did it, he would roast your behind." So pretty soon I erased this project from their mind.

On occasions, we had some soldiers get into difficulties like fist fights and a few things like that and it became a common practice that when we would report an incident to Colonel McNeeley that happened within the battalion, it got so that he would say, "You don't have to tell me where it occurred." And we'd say, "Why not, sir?" He'd say, "Obviously, it happened at Three Way Annie's." Now, I'll go no further with that other than to state there was a woman of the evening who had a house in Seaton and she apparently loved the soldiers and the soldiers apparently liked her. And, her name was Three Way Annie.

One day, a distinguished looking Britisher, well dressed and he had his monocle around his neck and his cane, came strolling into the battalion headquarters requesting to see the officer in command, the senior officer in command. Well, Colonel McNeeley was out, so I told the gentleman that Colonel McNeeley was out. I asked him if I could assist him. And he said, "Well, I have a complaint. You know, your troops are using the channel more or less as a firing range," which was true. We had devised a system of tossing tin cans out into the channel. We'd shoot at them to maintain our proficiency with the weapon. And this Britisher said, "All of that firing is disturbing the nesting season of my pheasants. Accordingly, I request that you move your firing range." Well, for a second, it went all over me. And I almost said, "But sir, don't you know a war is on?" But I held my tongue and told him I would consult with the battalion commander about it. And he departed. Well, Colonel McNeeley came in. I told him about the visitor we had and what he had said. And initially, Colonel Mac seemed to be shocked. And then he burst out and laughingly said, "Well by God, I believe that there will always be an England, as they say. Let's move the firing range," which we did. And that was a Britisher's approach. There is a war on but there are a lot of other things that you must consider. And one, to this gentleman, was the nesting season of his pheasants.

The training we underwent in England, before the D-Day was rather concentrated, we not only trained in the local areas but on occasion, we'd go to the moors. Now that's further from Seaton, a kind of badlands or wastelands and rather peculiar. It was covered with short grass and very little life existed on the moor. But it looked like it was solid ground all the way. But it was boggy in places and you'd be riding along in a vehicle and all of a sudden, all four wheels would go down. But this gave us some experience as to how to maneuver in that type of terrain. In addition, the division was ordered to go to Bronton, England, and undergo some training concentrating on how to eliminate pillboxes. Now the First Infantry Division was training at Bronton and I, among some other personnel, were designated to go to Bronton as liaison personnel and live with the First Infantry Division for a while and see what type training they were conducting and then, as the Fourth Division went to Bronton, we could use some of the techniques the First Division was using or alter it as we saw fit. So, I stayed with the First Infantry Division for several weeks and lived and trained with and observed the training of the Second Battalion, 16th Infantry. That battalion was commanded by Lieutenant Colonel Hicks and incidentally, he was a South Carolinian. I learned a great deal by watching the First Division train because, you know, they had already had combat experience and the Fourth Division had not. But during this association, I got a very good feel for what the training should be like. So, when the Fourth Division arrived, and the Second Battalion of the Eighth Regiment, my personnel and I were pretty well set. So, we had an extremely successful training period and really put the fine touches on the techniques and the tactics and the doctrine, the tactics and techniques used to breach a formidable position like pillboxes and even the Siegfried Line.

In addition, we had some extensive rehearsal training in amphibious operations at a place called Slapton Sands. This was also very profitable. But I recall one of the last exercises, kind of a dress rehearsal exercise which was conducted. Incidentally on these rehearsals, in that we were maneuvering in the English Channel, the German U-boats were always lurking about and attempting to sink some of our ships. As I say, on the last exercise, it was a real rehearsal exercise, we were supposed to land on the beaches at 6:30 in the morning. And incidentally, Slapton Sands had been selected as a practice amphibious landing site because there was an inundated area behind the beach that was very similar to the Utah Beach on which we would eventually land during D-Day. But no one at that time knew this, of course. Well, during this final rehearsal, one night, the night before we landed, some U-boats got inside the protective line of destroyers, which were protecting the beach head and our maneuver area, and sank an LCI, that was a landing craft, infantry. Thus, the Fourth Division suffered its first real casualties during the Slapton Sands operation. In addition, a German plane was shot down over the maneuver area and the Fourth Division captured its first two prisoners. But back to the exercise itself, the weather turned bad, and as I say, we were supposed to hit the beaches at say 7:00 a.m. And orders from higher headquarters were passed to delay the landing time for one hour. Well, when you have troops scattered all over an area in small craft riding around in circles waiting for H-Hour, you really can't be sure that every wave of craft received the word. Well, it happened in this case. The first and second waves, E & F Companies, received word that the H-Hour had been delayed one hour. G Company, the reserve company, failed to receive the radio transmission. Accordingly, at its appointed time to land, G Company charges in to the beach not knowing that H-Hour had been delayed. Well, Captain James W. "Chick" Haley, the company commander of G Company, he gets to shore and there's no one, no other soldiers preceding him and he knew there was something wrong but it was too late then, because by the time he landed and his soldiers had gotten on the beach pretty well, now comes the bombardment by rockets, naval gunfire softening up the simulated enemy position for the first wave to land. Well, rockets and mortars and naval gunfire fell all around G Company, in front of them, in the rear of them but fortunately not one man was injured. But we learned a lesson then and particularly the higher, the most senior officers learned a lesson that when one establishes H-Hour, it's very difficult to change that at the last minute. So, it is better to go on and let things run as directed. If not, you can really foul things up. And I'll mention this again later.

Now, I also had the opportunity to visit with the 101st Airborne Division. Now again, this was another liaison mission. The 101st Airborne Division had been designated to seize certain objectives inland on D-day and the seaborne forces, Fourth Division, were to link up quickly with elements of the 101st Airborne Division. I was designated, along with some others, to establish close liaison with members of the 101st. So, I visited the 101st and stayed with them for about, as I recall, six or seven days. And I was staying with the battalion and the battalion commanders name I don't recall right now, but I do know, I remember the regimental commander. It was Colonel Sink, later General Sink. And one night at dinner, Colonel Sink turned to me and began needling me about not being an airborne qualified individual. And so, I said, "Well Sir, I don't mind jumping out of a plane. It doesn't take a lot of guts or brains to do that." So, he seized on my comment and said, "Oh, you'll jump out of an aircraft, will you?" I said, "Yes sir, without any training." Well, in that I had made a statement, I wasn't going to back off, and he began to press it a little further. He said, "Very well then, tomorrow I'll let you make an airborne jump with us." I said, "Fine." So, he told the battalion commander and said, "In the morning, give him a little training on how to land and so forth and we'll take him up and let him jump." So that was agreeable with me and the next morning, I went down to this barn where some straw was on the floor and this sergeant gave me some instructions on how to hook up and stand in the door and jump out to hit on the side of the leg, roll and all that. I was all set. So, we got suited up and went up and we were flying around, and flying around and finally it was announced that the wind had gotten up so high that the jump had been canceled. So that night at dinner, Colonel Sink said, "Well, the weather was against us today but tomorrow night we're going to have a night jump." I said, "Well, I'm ready for that." After considering it a bit and some of the officers talked to Colonel Sink and Colonel Sink finally decided, "Well, I don't think we'd better let you try that because we're going to have a heavy equipment drop after the personnel drop and it would be just like you dumb infantrymen to have one of these heavy pieces of equipment come down and smack you right on top of the head. And I don't want to have to answer to Colonel Van Fleet on that." So, they did not permit me to jump and make the night jump.

While we were in England, General George S. Patton came to visit the Fourth Infantry Division. And the division, maybe I mentioned earlier, was scattered in various places. But for this occasion, the division was assembled near Exeter, where the regimental headquarters was located. Now with this particular day, extreme caution had been made that every man was lined up perfectly on the parade field. Now they had tape indicating the front rank and the left side of the rank and all this and much pains had gone into being sure that we had a perfect formation. Well, General Patton arrived and jumped up on the reviewing stand. All of a sudden, on the public address system, he announced everyone break ranks and come and to sit down around him. Well, my goodness, everybody in the division began to whooping and hollering, running toward the reviewing stand. Now this was indeed a surprise to everyone. And then he said, "Everybody sit down." And everyone sat down. And then he said, "Take off your combat helmet." And everyone removed their combat helmet. He waited a few minutes, looked over the entire crowd sitting there and he said, "I just want to see how many old bald-headed bastards you've got in the division." Well, a roar of laughter, whistling and clapping of the hands resulted therefrom. Then he started his little speech. And he was giving us a real fiery pep talk about fighting the Nazis and he finally said this, "Now when we get over there, we're going to fight them tooth and toenail. And we're going to fight regardless of what happens, even if you run out of ammunition, we're going to still fight them. We can use the 'blivid' gun." And there was a pause and he said, "You know what the 'blivid' gun is, don't you?" And there was still silence and he said, "The 'blivid' gun is when you take off your sock and punch holes in it and shit in it and then sailing it around your head." Well, you could imagine what happened then. Everybody roared with laughter and many were shocked, as I was.

D-Day

Now Brigadier General Teddy Roosevelt joined the Fourth Division as an assistant division commander. Now there's a long story behind this, but suffice it so say, that General Roosevelt did not have a command, but he wanted to land on D-Day with some organization. And he selected the Fourth Infantry Division and selected the Second Battalion, the Eighth Regiment as the unit organization he wanted to land with. Therefore, he spent much time with the Second Battalion and became very close friends to Colonel McNeeley. And I also considered him a very close friend. He was a real soldier's general. For example, the men in the H-Hour would be working on the boat loading tables at 12-1 o'clock in the morning. General Roosevelt would come in wearing a knit cap. Now this was a little old knit cap that fitted under the helmet liner to keep the head warm. And it was authorized head gear but not by itself. The helmet or helmet liner was supposed to be worn over it. Strict orders were you never wore this knit by itself. Well, General Roosevelt wore that knit cap by itself irrespective of the orders. But he would come in and see me slaving over boat loading tables, whether I had them organized properly, with the proper number of engineers, for example, and the boat and the number of explosives they would need and the type vehicle they would have and infantrymen as protection for the engineers. And he would sit down with his walking stick, he always carried his walking stick, and lean over and look at me and he'd say, "George, what are you looking so worried about?" I said, well sir, I'm just concerned about when we do make this invasion, we've got to have everything just right, particularly in the first, second, and third waves." He said, "Aw, don't worry about that." He said, "You could put anybody in those boats and we're going to get ashore and stay there, so don't worry so much. Let's have a cup of coffee." And we'd drink coffee and he would relieve the tension and then he'd tell some humorous stories about what happened to him on various occasions and Colonel Mac would end the conversation. Pretty soon, the pressure was gone. Well, when they'd leave, I'd go back and work some more. But it was good to have him around. I'll tell you more about him later.

Now, we were finally moved to Torquay and everyone knew that we were approaching the day of reckoning, so to speak, because when we got to Torquay, we were put in the compound that had barbwire fences around it, security guards around it and no one was permitted to leave or enter that compound except by special pass. About this time, Colonel McNeeley told me that he wanted me to go away with him to a big briefing one day. So, I went with him and I don't even recall where the meeting was held. But we got there and I was trying to get in with Colonel McNeeley along with Colonel Van Fleet and General Barton and others. And I was just a little captain. I found out that I would have to have special permission to get in to this high-level meeting. Eventually, Colonel McNeeley, Colonel Van Fleet and General Barton got permission and they said from General Eisenhower, but I know General Bradley got involved. So, I got into the briefing. And it was an ultra-secret briefing, because this was the final briefing prior to the actual invasion on D-Day, in Normandy. Now I shall never forget the tremendous number of maps, detailed maps of exactly what the Air Force was going to do, what the Navy was going to do, and then they began to talk about what the army forces were going to do and down to the exact portion of the beach where each assault would land. And I was the only captain in this audience that I could see. But I saw many, many generals and here, I recalled this, that a British admiral got up and I remembered his name for years, but right now I just can't think of it, got up and he began to talk about what happened at the Slapton Sands exercise. And he said he made a gross mistake and that he permitted a British destroyer to fall out of formation, which was protecting the up-maneuver area, and never followed up to see that another ship took its place and the U-boats came and then sank the LCI. And he was really upset about it. And General Eisenhower and other general officers got up later and told him this was just one of those things and for him not to worry about it and tried to calm his concern, but later he committed suicide. During this briefing, everyone was warned not once, but at least three times, that no one was to talk about what they had seen and heard this particular day and it was just ultra-secret. Well, this impressed me a great deal but what really impressed me was the details of where ships all would be, what ports they would load at and how they would assemble, and the protection we had, the Air Force protection, the bombardment by bombing and strafing by the Air Force would take place and then the Navy would fire on the beaches with their destroyers and battleships and then, seaborne forces would come ashore and all this , having been preceded by the airborne drops of the 82nd and 101st Airborne Divisions. But it was a real detailed briefing. So, we left there, came back to our compound at Torquay.

Now, in the meantime, every night old Axis Salley would get on the radio and tell us, members of the Fourth Division, we know where you are and look out, we're going to get you when you try to invade and maybe we'll get you before you have an invasion, and so forth. Well, we got back to the compound at Torquay and determined that Colonel McNeeley, after he and I had received this detailed briefing, that we should sleep in a tent together and have a guard walking around the tent at a distance, in case either he or I talked in our sleep so no one could overhear it. And this sentry walked around far enough so he could not hear any words in case we talked in our sleep.

Now one particular night, Colonel McNeeley and I had turned in for the night and he was sleeping in his cot and about to go to sleep and I was over in my cot on the other side of the tent and the sirens in Torquay went off announcing a German raid was coming. And naturally people began to run and scurry and jump in the trenches, protective trenches we had dug in the compound area. And Colonel Mac finally said, "George, you think we ought to go hit the trenches?" I said, "No sir, Colonel Mac, they're not going to bomb up here." Well the sirens kept going and pretty soon the anti-aircraft guns opened up and then we could hear bombs falling down near the port in Torquay and it began to get closer and closer and pretty soon a stick of bombs started falling. One, the last one, hit about 150 yards from the compound. At that time, Colonel Mac and I both went out of the side of the tent and running for the trenches. Well, I dived over in the trench and there were so many people in it, I bounced up off of them about a foot off the ground. So, I said to heck with this so I just laid down on top of the ground. I don't know where Colonel Mac finally found a place. It just so happened the bombs cut off right within 150 yards of the edge of the compound. Pretty soon, an all-clear signal was given. So I meekly got off the ground, sneaked back into the tent and jumped in my cot. After a while, Colonel Mac comes in. He didn't say a word, climbed in his bunk on his cot and about 15 minutes passed. Then he says, "George." I said, "Yes sir." He said, "Remind me to never believe a damn thing you say, OK." I said, "OK, yes sir," and that was the end of that transmission.

Eventually, all personnel of the battalion were briefed on where we would land on D-day morning and were shown specific tasks and objectives assigned each assault team, company and battalion. Once this was accomplished, security of the compound at Torquay became even stricter. As I recall, we had only one man within the battalion administer his self-inflicted wound to avoid combat. He did this by shooting himself in the foot.

During one meeting of officers of the 101st Airborne Division and the Fourth Infantry Division, I remember Colonel Sink chiding Colonel Van Fleet a bit by saying, "Be sure, Van, that members of the Eighth Regiment hurry and make contact with my troops at the causeways, which crossed inundated area behind the beaches because we have other objectives to capture." Colonel Van Fleet's reply was, Bob, you just be sure your troops get there because mine certainly will be there."

The Second Battalion was marching down through Torquay late at night and loading aboard the APA Barnett and General Roosevelt was standing beside the street and I remember very vividly one of the companies were coming by and there was a tall man who walked by. He had the mortar, the tube of an 81 mm mortar on his back. And behind him was a short soldier, small of stature and he had the big baseplate of the mortar on his back. And General Roosevelt tapped his cane on the ground and said, "Isn't that typical? The big man always gets the small load and the little man always gets the big load." And this little soldier who was carrying the baseplate, he hunched that thing on his shoulder a little higher and said, "That is right, General, but we can take it. Can't we?" And General Roosevelt laughed and I did as well as everybody else. But this was just the typical type comment that General Roosevelt would make. He loved soldiers and he, as I said earlier, he was a soldier's general.

As the column of troops went silently down through town, I fell back to the tail of the column to be sure that we'd gotten everybody. And I was walking along, behind the last element of the battalion, and an elderly British civilian fell in behind me. And of course, I didn't know who he was but I assumed that he must have had something to do with the security force, the British security force, and as we turned to go down to the ramp, where we were getting in small boats and being transported out to the APA, this gentleman said to me, "Good luck to you, laddie." I didn't turn around, I just nodded my head and continued to move down toward the loading area. But he, having said that, I knew that he knew this was the real thing. And it also brought to my mind that, yep, good luck to me, but I didn't know whether I'd ever see England or the United States again because my philosophy, at this time, was a little unusual, I suppose, because before I left the United States, I told my wife not to expect to see me coming home. And I thought about that, this particular night, just a little bit because honestly and truthfully, I didn't think I would live to return to the United States. I suppose the reason I felt this way is number one, I knew people were going to get killed. There was just no question in my mind about that. And second, I have always tended to be one who was more or less out in front, so to speak. I never asked any soldier to do anything that I would not willingly do myself. And third, I didn't want to clutter my mind with any thoughts that might inhibit me in any way. In other words, I had come to fight. And I was going to do my best to fight and think about accomplishment of mission rather than self-preservation. Now don't misunderstand me. I would not take unnecessary chances because we had been trained to take advantage of cover and concealment and always protect oneself, but at the same time, we were taught to accomplish the mission, that the mission was of utmost importance, even above life itself.

One-night, General Roosevelt, Colonel McNeeley and several others were sitting around just talking late at night and I remember something that General Roosevelt said that I never forgot. He was talking about World War I. And he said that on occasion, that we would get so tired while fighting this war that we were about to become engaged in, that there would be a tendency, on occasion, to stand up and bare one's chest and stretch out one's arms and say, "Come on and kill me." And he said, "Now you better believe this is going to happen. But when it does, that is the time to be especially careful. Be very cautious about taking adequate cover to protect oneself because you're so tired, your rationale has left you." And on occasion in combat, I thought about that. And on many occasions, I felt like doing just what General Roosevelt said. And when those feelings came to me, I would think about what he said and take extra precaution, not to the extent that I would not accomplish my mission, but being a little more careful. That's the same thing as sometimes you get so tired of marching and fighting that you don't think you could put one foot in front of the other. But you just try it. Put one foot in front of the other and pretty soon, you've regained your second wind, so to speak, and something will come along to cause the adrenaline to flow again and you can make it. So never give up. Never give up hope because one without hope, in my opinion, is a lost soul.

Returning now to the APA Barnett upon which was loaded the Second Battalion, 8th Infantry reinforced. Now I might explain the term "reinforced." In addition to the battalion itself, we had some anti-aircraft units from the 101st Airborne Division aboard the APA because it had been agreed that these anti-aircraft guns of the 101st Division would come ashore with us and later would rejoin the 101st Airborne Division. In addition to that, and as an integral part of the reinforcements of the Second Battalion, 8th Regiment, we had engineers because they were supposed to assist us in employing explosives to breach gaps through the tetrahedron, which were angle irons placed in the water to preclude boats from landing and also to breach holes in the sea wall so vehicles could get through once we were on the beaches. And one of my chores as the S3 of the battalion was to ensure that those engineers had spaces in the LCVP's along with the infantrymen and personnel who had been designated to assist the engineers in getting their explosives to the appropriate place at the proper time on the beaches. I might pause here also and state that Brigadier General Teddy Roosevelt, Jr. and his aide, Stevie, was also aboard because as mentioned earlier, General Roosevelt had requested of General Eisenhower, which was approved, that General Roosevelt would land with the first wave of a battalion which he selected , and he selected the Second Battalion, Eighth Regiment, Fourth Division as the Battalion he would like to accompany ashore on D-Day and H-Hour.

Now soon after boarding the APA, I learned that the first lieutenant of the ship, of the ship's crew, of the ship in fact, was a fellow I had attended, Presbyterian College with. And he had graduated a year or two before I did, but I knew him well because he had been a member of the Presbyterian College boxing team. His name was John Wilkes Todd from Lauren, South

Carolina. Even though we did not have a Navy ROTC unit at PC, somehow John Wilkes had obtained a commission in the U.S. Navy after he graduated from PC. Now as I recall, we were set to sail or set to cross, steam out of port and cross the channel the night of June 4, but due to extremely bad weather, the decision by General Eisenhower was made that the D-Day and H-Hour would be delayed until the morning of June 6, 6:30 a.m. in the morning for the Second Battalion, Eighth Regiment at least. So, on the night of June 4, when we loaded, we pulled out of the port but then the orders were changed to hold off, and either go back to port or stay in anchor off the coast until further orders.

Well, the orders came on June 5 so on the late evening or early night of June 5, checking and rechecking my boat loading tables to be sure that everything was set. Here I might explain that we had some LCVP's, now that's landing craft, the vehicle and personnel, aboard the APA Barnett, but not nearly enough to satisfy our requirements. Therefore, when the APA Barnet anchored in the rendezvous area early that morning, additional LCVP's and LCM's, which is landing craft mechanized, were to be discharged from other designated ships and come along side the APA to accept their personnel cargo, weapons and small vehicles, etc. in order for the personnel of the Second Battalion to have sufficient craft in which to load. Now in order for the personnel to get into these craft that would come alongside the APA, the soldiers would have to climb down rope nets which would be lowered over the side of the APA. Well, the LCVP's which were aboard the APA, they could be rail loaded. In other words, loaded at deck level, all you had to do was just step over in the boat, in the landing craft and once it got full with the proper number of personnel and the equipment, then it would be lowered into the water and thence they would join their respective boat team wave.

Sometime before midnight, the lieutenant aboard ship, John Wilkes Todd, came to me about the amount of equipment that some of the soldiers were abandoning. And he indicated there was quite a lot of equipment and impediment being discarded aboard ship. So, I figured it out pretty quickly and told him that yes, I anticipated that and in fact had contributed because we had been issued these assault vests, which were something new, and initially they looked like they would be a great piece of equipment. On the other hand, with so many pockets in them, there was a great temptation to just add things to the pockets, which I had done along with other soldiers. As the time approached for us to land on the H-Hour, it became quite obvious that we had overloaded ourselves and it was about time to get rid of some of this excess baggage and creature comforts we had stuffed our pockets with. Accordingly, he and I went below decks and selected a compartment and then made an announcement over the public address system that anyone who had any piece of equipment or items to be discarded, take it to this particular compartment so we would not litter the ship because the APA was destined to become a hospital transport ship after we had departed therefrom.

Now during the daylight hours, Colonel McNeeley was checking through the ship and he discovered that a couple of members of the U.S. Army news media had been given some homing pigeons by some press members while in England. And these individuals had these homing pigeons aboard ship. Apparently, what they were going to do is try to get a scoop on the news of our landing. And what they had planned to do once we got ashore was release the pigeons to which were attached capsules, including a message to the effect that the troops had landed. Well, Colonel McNeeley found out about this and he confiscated these homing pigeons and had them securely locked in the brig and left orders with the captain of the APA not to let anyone get at those pigeons until the afternoon of June 6th at the earliest.

About 2:00 a.m. on the morning of June 6th, I went up on deck because I knew, according to the schedule, the 82nd and the 101st Airborne Divisions would soon be dropping on the peninsula. Well, I didn't have to wait long. In just a few seconds after I reached the deck, the German anti-aircraft fire commenced. And I just can't describe what this thing looked like. They were shooting tracers and the tracers were crisscrossing in the sky and the entire sky was just lit up with all this ack ack (anti-aircraft artillery). And the old expression that ack ack was so thick you could step out of the plane and walk on it appeared to be an accurate summation of this one. Well, I've seen Fourth of July celebrations and other things, but I never have ever seen anything like that. And I hope never to see anything like that again. Well, it was rather an awesome sight. And we felt rather small and insignificant and very lonely out there in the darkness and on the channel and bouncing up and down in these waves and the sky above you and there in front of you they're all lit up with these tracers. Pretty soon, it got even worse.

A German plane began dropping chandelier flares, we called them that because they hung up there so long. And first, the first pass he made, he dropped some to our right front and next, to the left front of us. And next was directly ahead. And pretty soon he'd dropped some well behind us. And when those chandelier flares lit up, we just knew that they had spotted us. Now we're talking about a real lonely feeling, a helpless feeling, that really caught me. But fortunately, they never did drop any right over us. And apparently the angle and the light emitting from these chandelier flares was not sufficient to cause accurate pictures to be taken by the plane. Now on the other hand, accurate pictures could have been taken but, in order to process them, this may have taken too long a time. I mean, we would already be ashore by the time they were developed. But whatever happened, we were not subjected to bombing or strafing, fortunately, at this stage of the game.

Soon after reaching the rendezvous area, LCVP's and LCM's from other ships began arriving alongside the APA to be loaded. Therefore, I went topside to supervise the loading of these craft. When we were ready to commence the loading into the small craft, a naval officer on the APA, using my boat loading tables, would announce over the public address system the LCVP number and wave number which that LCVP would be a part of. In addition, he would announce the boat loading for the particular boat team. This was the signal for that particular boat team leader to lead his boat team members from their designated compartments on the APA up to the proper loading position. Here I might say that this procedure went smoothly as silk. However, we ran into trouble when the men began climbing down the rope nets. As I mentioned earlier, the channel was extremely rough that morning. And it was cold. So, water was extremely cold. Soldiers with rifles on their backs and packs and what not, were climbing down this cold, slippery wet net, attempting to enter the small LCVP's. Bouncing up and down in the channel was quite a chore. And it was pitch black dark. Unfortunately, I saw on two occasions, just before the men were to turn loose and try to jump in the small LCVP, a foot would get hung in the net and the man would be hanging upside down and the LCVP would go out of sight and then come straight out from nowhere and smacked the soldier on the shoulders and head. Even though I was using a flashlight on occasion, it didn't help. Personnel already loaded in the boat would try to lessen the shock by catching the man and pushing him up and try to loosen his foot or equipment. I saw this happen at least twice, and it could have happened many more times. But the thing that really concerned me was all of a sudden, you'd see small landing craft way up high on a wave to almost half the distance up to the rail of the APA. And the next second, it would be down in the trough so far that it would be impossible to see with the naked eye even dimly with the flashlight. But in spite of this, we successfully loaded the small craft.

Now knowing the boat number in which General Roosevelt would be loaded, as his boat number was approaching to be announced, I ran back down into his compartment where he and his aide, Stevie, were, to alert General Roosevelt that his boat team number would be coming up pretty soon. I dashed in and told General Roosevelt that his boat team number would be called very shortly and that his boat was being rail loaded. And he thanked me and then hollered at Stevie. He said, "Stevie, bring me a life belt." Now, I remind you that every one who was going to participate in the invasion had to wear a life belt. It was a rubber belt in which some capsules had been placed and if you got in trouble, you just mashed or squeezed on a certain portion of the belt and these capsules would be punctured and air would be inflated or air would inflate the life belt. Well, when General Roosevelt hollered, "Stevie, where is my life belt?", Stevie said, "General, I don't know, I've already given you three." And General Roosevelt said, "Dammit, I don't care how many you've given me. I don't have one now." So. Stevie and I dashed around, found one and gave it to him.

General Roosevelt had a little smile on his face as we were walking down the alley, galley way or "alley way,". I think he called it, preparing to walk up the ladder, a stairway to…land level, and I said, "General Roosevelt, do you have your weapon and your pistol and all of your ammunition?" He stopped, turned around and looked at me and says, "George," while he patted his shoulder holster pistol, "Yep, I've got my pistol and I've got six rounds of ammunition." I said, "Sir, don't you want more ammunition than that?" he said, "No, six rounds will do me just fine. I don't need any more than six rounds." I said, "Very well, sir." And so he walked on up the ladder with his walking cane and got to a rail where he was going to load and, even though I say it was rail loaded, the LCVP had been put over the side of the ship and you had to jump down, about four or five feet into the LCVP. And General Roosevelt climbed up on the edge of the APA and was about to jump in and some soldier reached up, grabbed his hand from inside the boat and said, "Here, General, let me help you." General Roosevelt took his walking stick and lightly tapped him on the arm and says, "Get out of my way, I can jump in there myself. I'm not a cripple, you know." Well, even under all this stress and strain, the people laughed and General Roosevelt jumped in the boat, followed by Stevie. And they went with one of the boats from E Company, which would constitute one half of the first wave.

We finally loaded everybody. And Colonel McNeeley, the battalion commander, and I along with several other members of Headquarters Company, Second Battalion. We also included a little fellow by the name of Smokey David, in our LCVP which was rail loaded, too. Well, we were in what they call a free boat. The battalion commander's boat could go anywhere he wanted to and not confined to a particular wave. But in the plans, we had, Colonel McNeeley had decided to land behind the third wave. Now the first wave was E and F Company and then G Company and then H Company and then other companies behind like headquarters and Headquarters Company and so forth. But we had determined to land behind G Company and possibly in the third wave so we could kind of see how things were going when we hit the beaches, and we could see how E Company and F Company and G Company were fairing. And if any changes needed to be made, then Colonel McNeeley would be on the spot and I, as the S-3, would be there too to assist in passing orders if we wanted anything changed, such as G Company taking over from F or taking over from E if E or F suffered excessive casualties. So now comes the circling in the blackout conditions by boats which constituted waves, or portion of a wave. And there was a control boat handled by the Navy that would ride along and, using a megaphone, he would holler out, "What wave is this?" The response would come back, "E Company, first wave," "F Company, First Wave," and so forth. Colonel Mac and I attached ourselves initially to the wave of G Company. As I mentioned two or three times, the channel was extremely rough. We're pitching up and down, circling. The fumes from these LCVP's would normally make anyone sick as a pup. In fact, in Slapton Sands' rehearsal, large number of troops got sick. And I got sick. And all you did was take off your helmet and take out your helmet liner and fill it full and then dump it over the side and then get ready to refill it. Well, this particular morning I don't recall having seen one man get sick because of the tension and excitement that was just built up in us. But it's a wonder, maybe I'll say, believe it or not, there must be something to this thing that seasickness is caused by the mind rather than any other thing, mind over matter.

Well, we continued to circle in this churning water until just before daylight and began the run toward the beach. Now this was a considerable distance we had to go, and I forget exactly how far, but it was a good distance. We could see, in the early light of morning, the shoreline but could make out no features. But everybody's eyes were strained toward the beaches because we had studied the maps and the models which had been made in the United States. And here is a kind of a story within itself: Portions of the actual landing beaches had been made in various places throughout the United States and then assembled piece by piece while we were in England. This was done so that any person working on a small block of the actual beaches could not determine what part of the world it was located in. Well, we'd studied these and so we knew where pillboxes were located and what the sea wall looked like and there were some distinguishing landmarks that I was looking for in particular. One was a tower and another looked like an old wind mill tower. But for some reason, we couldn't make it out as we were approaching the beaches.

Now I might pause here to say also that I mentioned earlier about the mine sweepers. The mine sweepers had supposedly swept a lane toward the beach. An underwater demolition team, men swimming in scuba diving equipment were supposed to have blown some tetrahedron and barbwire that was put in the water by the Germans as protective measures. Now the tetrahedron were made of steel like railroad ties. It looked like jackstone, a large jackstone and they would just line the beach. At high tide, an LCVP would have difficulty in landing because of these things. But we were going to land at mid tide knowing that these tetrahedron would interfere with us. We were going to land at mid tide so that we could pass through tetrahedron and barbwire on foot rather than have the LCVP's and other landing craft become fouled in the barbwire and the tetrahedron. Also, the Navy had provided two boats that would mark the width of the space through which our assault craft would pass.

And as light began to improve with the passing of time that morning, the first casualty I saw was one of these Navy boats apparently had hit a mine. And the boat was up turned and one Navy man was sitting on the bottom of the boat and holding on to another man who was obviously in critical condition or dead. Soon after passing this boat, I was looking to my left rear and I saw a large transport type ship hit a mine. That ship went up in the air, its nose up out of the water and rocked very seriously to the starboard and to the port side. During this rocking motion, you could see men jumping off the ship into the channel. This continued as long as I could watch it. You could see personnel jumping off the ship. It was later determined that this ship, on this ship was elements of the 29th Field Artillery Battalion of the Fourth Infantry Division. In fact, the 29th Field Artillery Battalion was the one that normally gave close fire support to the Eight Regiment. But I still have a vivid picture in my mind of the results of this tremendous explosion resulting from the mine that caused this ship to appear to come up out of the water at least halfway the length of the ship and then buck like a bucking horse and wallowing back left and right into the water and personnel and people jumping off this wounded ship, into the channel.

Now about this time, the bombers began to strafe, bomb the beaches. And that was a sight to see as wave after wave of bombers came parallel to the beach and were dropping their strings of bombs. Smoke and dust and dirt just obliterated the area. But now we couldn't even see the shoreline, let alone, try to pick out any distinguishing features that we had memorized. So, this continued for quite awhile as we were approaching the beach and then, as the bombers went away, the naval gunfire opened up. Oh, I might mention this, when these bombers were parallel to the beaches, I looked up and was looking at a formation of planes and a bomber on the left flank of the formation and then it exploded in mid-air. And I didn't think too much about it other than I wondered what caused the explosion. It was probably German anti-aircraft fire. After World War II, the Lieutenant Mowese I spoke about when I was discussing my experiences at Fort Benning, Georgia, in 1940, happened to be a member of that flight. And after World War II, we got to talking about the bombing on D-Day and he knew that the Eighth Regiment was down below preparing to land. But I didn't know he was in the air. But I mentioned to him, having seen this bomber explode in midair, and he said, "By golly, I was in that flight and I was looking at the same time at that bomber."

Now the battleships opened up their naval gunfire bombardment and they began to pulverize the beaches and behind the beaches. In addition, rocket ships began to fire and discharge their rockets toward the beaches.

So, there was plenty of noise going on and plenty of smoke in the area. As we got closer to the beach, a ME109, a German fighter plane, came out from behind some clouds and was diving, it appeared to me, to be directly at our particular landing craft, the free boat the Colonel McNeeley and we were in. Right behind that ME109 came a British spitfire and the British spitfire fired three bursts of machine-gun, p-r-r-r-t, p-r-r-r-t, p-r-r-r-t. And the German ME109 just disintegrated in the air and the propeller fell right in front of our LCVP. All I could do was look up, make a sign, thank you fellow Britisher.

While all this was going on, the coxswain, the navy man who was piloting our small landing craft, began to fall back and get further and further behind the position that Colonel McNeeley and I wanted to be in. So, Colonel Mac hollered back and told him to speed up. Well, this young fellow speeded up a little bit and then slowed down. About this time, we began to go past some of the D-Day tanks which were accompanying us on this invasion. Now I'll have to pause and describe what I'm talking about. The 70th Tank Battalion had worked very closely with the Eighth Infantry Regiment and while in England, someone devised a method of floating these tanks. Now what they did was put a propeller shaft on the rear of the tank and then constructed a rubberized portion that when pulled up, would extend above the turret and hopefully preventing water from getting over the tank and down into the turret. Now these tanks had been discharged from LCM's, I believe, or maybe a larger landing craft, about…I think about 800 or 900 yards from the beach. And these tanks were supposed to propel themselves forward until they reached bottom or shoreline and then just crawl right on up on the beaches. Well, this was a very ingenious idea. Unfortunately, they didn't work too well in the rough channel. They would have been fine on a mill pond. But the channel was so rough that morning that these tanks couldn't steer themselves very well. So, they were kind of wallowing along the sea and every once in a while, you would see one start to sink. And they had a rubber raft aboard each one and you'd see the tank crewmen pull out the rubber raft, inflate it, then jump on it and get away from the tank and the tank would sink.

Now as we were passing the company commander's tank, this particular thing happened. The rubber raft was pulled up and the crew bailed out into the rubber raft except the company commander. And the company commander started to come out of the turret of the tank and then all of a sudden, he didn't make it. The tank began to sink and pretty soon the company commander with the tank, disappeared. Well, in looking back we did not see him come to the surface. So, I assumed that he would have drowned. Well, to continue the story about him, later I found out from him personally that as he was trying to get out of the turret of the tank, his foot got hung on something inside the tank. So, he couldn't get out and just went down with the tank and doubled himself up, finally loosened his foot and came to the surface. One of the landing craft which had discharged its personnel on the beach, came by, picked him up and took him back to a hospital ship. And he was evacuated to England for a short period of time under observation and then joined us later on the peninsula. And I recall very well when he reported to duty. I had quite a shock when I saw him because I thought to be sure he had drowned.

Now back to the LCVP, when Colonel McNeeley for the third time told this coxswain to speed it up and this young fellow would speed it up a little bit and then slow down again. Colonel Mac finally went back and pulled his pistol and told this young fellow that he meant to get going and to take off. Well, this young fellow understood that when he saw that pistol. So, he really moved out. We went through the third wave and now we were really traveling fast. And I was trying to pick up landmarks. And the bombing which the shoreline had been subjected to had apparently knocked down the few landmarks that I was looking for. But we figured there was something wrong. First, the terrain of the beach itself didn't look right. It appeared that we were landing too far to the left because at a great distance, we could see the mouth of the Murderet River and we were supposed to be landing about almost 1,000 yards to the right of where we were landing. But we could do nothing about it now. So, we kept charging toward the beach and Colonel Mac did not ask this fellow to slow down after having prodded him enough to cause him to go faster. As we approached the beaches, the pillboxes became clearer visually and the tetrahedron stood out like bristles on a hog's back.

And we landed right behind the second wave. Now that was elements of E and F Company. So, as we were, just as the bottom of the landing craft touched the ground, this coxswain just dropped the ramp. And he wasn't going any further. Well, men began to jump off the right and left corners of the ramp as we'd been taught to, and right ahead of me was this short little fellow by the name of Smokey David. Well, Smokey jumped off the right corner of the ramp and disappeared. So, seeing this, I jumped more or less to the front of the ramp, which we weren't trained to do but I said I'm not going to jump there. And when I hit the bottom, came up, the water was up around my neck. And people began to jump behind me, seeing what happened to Smokey David. They jumped in the direction I had gone. I looked back out in the channel and all of a sudden Smokey David's bald head appeared out behind the LCVP. Apparently, he had jumped in a hole possibly made by a landing craft or just a quirk of nature. But he had gone down and gone under the landing craft and back out into the channel. How he missed the prop or the screw of the landing craft I'll never know. But while under water, he had begun to shed his equipment and his helmet and everything else. And all that was showing was his bald head. Well, he began swimming toward the beach.

And then we began to move through this water up to our necks toward the beach. Now we'd been trained that once you hit the beach, you run across that thing. Never lie down on the beach and don't crowd up against the sea wall when you get there. You've got to push on inland. That was drilled into us. Well, while walking through that water dragging along, we met with something we had to reckon with. To our left was Pointe du Hoc. Now Pointe du Hoc was right adjacent to the Murderete River and it stuck out in a real point. The Germans had artillery batteries honeycombed in that point. The Rangers, U.S. Ranger Battalion, was supposed to take that point and they had difficulty because it was a sheer cliff. So, this artillery, the German artillery and mortars from Pointe du Hoc was raking the beaches. Now E Company and F Company and G Company had been issued a black rocket, one black rocket each, to fire when they wanted U.S. naval gunfire to lift from the beaches and shift inland. Now I saw one of the black rockets call off in E Company area. And later, I saw an F Company rocket go off. And as we were coming to shore, the artillery from Pointe du Hoc, the Germany artillery from Pointe du Hoc was, as I say, just raking the beach. And what I began to do, and other fellows around me saw what I was doing and did the same thing, when we'd hear a shell coming or projectile coming through the air, just ducked down under the water and let it splatter all over the top and them come up and try to run again. Now this helped a great deal, it appeared to me. But pretty soon, we got in the water about waist deep and less than that and the only thing you could do was just try to run. And I emphasize *try*. The water in the channel was so cold that our muscles had become cramped. And you'd run about six or seven paces and there was no way you could go any further so we'd hit the beach and lie there a second or two and get up and try to run again.

Now while this was going on, there was a man in front of me from I believe F Company. And he had a cloverleaf 81mm mortar ammunition on his shoulder. Now the reason he had that is we had designated certain individuals to bring additional mortar rounds ashore so that our 81mm mortars would have enough ammunition to support us with. So this man was to drop this ammunition at the sea wall and then when H Company, that had a 81 mm mortar platoon, came ashore, they would run down to the sea wall and gather up this ammunition for their use. Well, as we were struggling to cross the beach, I was standing up at the time and this man was too, trying to run. A mortar round, German mortar round, came in and hit this soldier right in the top of his head. That caused the 81 mm mortar rounds to detonate also. And this man's body just completely disappeared. I felt something hit me on the left thigh, just above my groin, and I looked down and this thumb was the only thing I could see left of him. Bits of flesh were scattered everywhere and some on my clothing but his thumb was the only discernable part of a human being that you could see left. Another thing is there was a human stomach on the beach. Now why it was there and what happened, I don't know. But it was quite obvious that is was a human stomach. And that was all.

Just before getting to the sea wall, two other things happened. Many of our soldiers began hollering, "Get the naval gunfire to shift." And it didn't take me long to figure out what was happening. From Pointe de Hoc, where the German artillery was firing from, if you didn't look carefully and listen carefully, it sounded like the rounds that were hitting among us was coming from the channel. But actually, it was coming from Pointe du Hoc, because our naval gunfire had already shifted. But in that the troops were hollering, "Get that naval gunfire off our backs," I ran over to G Company, saw a man, got him to holler to fire the black rocket again, which was done. But this German artillery kept raking the beaches and I'm sure that there were some soldiers, former soldiers living today, who think that our naval gunfire was falling amongst us. And that is not so. It was that artillery and mortar fire coming from Pointe du Hoc. In addition, there was artillery, German artillery coming from our front but the one that was really giving us a fit was from Pointe du Hoc.

Now just before I got out of the water safely, at the edge of the water, mid tide as I mentioned earlier, a Corporal Speck, he had been one of my baseball pitchers, was lying on the beach. He'd been hit in both legs and I ran by and reached down and started to pull him and he said, "No, no. Don't touch me." So, I stopped and I said, "I'm going to help you, Speck." He said, "No sir, your place is inland. Leave me alone and get going." An so I did. Now later, I thought Speck died. Now whether he was hit again or whether at the tide, being mid tide, continued to roll in and he was drowned, I don't know. But I would assume he was hit again because there were enough medical personnel who came in later, seeing an individual in this kind of condition, I think they would have detected it and evacuated him. But that was a tough thing to leave that man there but he insisted and kept telling me not to touch him, and my place was inland. Years later I was told Corporal Speck had actually survived so possibly medical personnel or a medical aid man saw Speck and as able to evacuate him before he was hit again or drowned.

Before reaching the sea wall, it became apparent to me that we had landed 800 to 1,000 yards further left than intended because where we landed there was not as many tetrahedron as was further up the beach. In addition, we were closer to the mouth of the Murderet River than we expected to be plus the fact that there was much more barbwire in the water because they had not put as many tetrahedron down there. They had supplemented it. They had replaced it with barbwire. In addition, there was mud in the bottom along the beach which indicated that we were pretty close to the mouth of the Murderet River. Looking back on it, the mistake had occurred because of a failure to properly calculate the effect the weather would have on the landing craft or specifically, how fast the tide was running back that morning in the channel. Normally, the Navy was very accurate in calculating drift of craft which would occur as a result of tide. But this particular morning the channel was so rough that the calculation was somewhat off. So that is what happened. We just drifted too far to the left because of the running tide. But I think it was lucky in one respect. We did not land head on against two rather formidable pillboxes. We were slightly to the left of them, so we could attack them from an angle rather than head on. In this connection, I did not see this but was told later that when the ramp was dropped on one LCVP, a German machine gunner in the pillbox opened fire and killed an officer and three men before they could get out of the landing craft.

Now General Roosevelt, having landed with the first wave in E Company, had made his way to the sea wall and I saw him a brief moment further up the beach walking along, waving his walking cane and encouraging troops to keep moving.

The incident I shall now describe was told to me. I did not see this happen but I believe it definitely did happen. It concerns the platoon leader of E Company by the name of Lt. Rebarchek. While he was wading ashore in neck deep water, he began to try and contact his company commander, Captain Lees, on the little hand held 536 radio that we had been issued. And he tried unsuccessfully for several times and so by the time he had waded ashore where he was waist deep in the water, Captain Lees saw Rebarcheck turn toward the channel and heave the 536 radio back out into the channel and then turned and started crossing the beach with his particular boat team. Later, Captain Lees asked…. Lieutenant Rebarchek in my presence why he did do such a thing. Lieutenant Rebarcek replied and said, "Well, when I turned on my radio, I could hear nothing but BBC broadcasting that troops were ashore on the shores of France. And here, knowing that we were the first troops to land, and that all of us were in water neck deep or waist deep, I just decided the heck with this and turned and threw that away. I couldn't get anybody on it. I was trying to contact you, Captain Lees, and I just became frustrated and tossed it back into the channel."

Colonel McNeeley and I devised a scheme of maneuver for the invasion of D-Day. E and F Company were to land abreast on the beach and proceed directly inland. The terrain behind the beach consisted of sand dunes and then continued for approximately a half mile. And then one would reach an inundated area, a very low ground which had been flooded with water. And there were three causeways crossing this inundation. Seizure of these three causeways were very vital because if the Germans were to blow or destroy these causeways and launch a counterattack against us while we were on the land between the beach and the inundated area, we could be in very serious trouble. Accordingly, E and F Company, attacking abreast, were to reach the inundated area opposite two causeways, number two and three, seize those causeways, then turn left and proceed to the left toward causeways number one. G Company, landing behind E and F Company, was to follow E and F Company inland for a few hundred yards, then turn left and proceed down the beach, clearing up pillboxes and any enemy, then turn right and seize causeway number one, which was near the little village of Pouppeville. Colonel McNeeley was to follow E Company and I would follow G Company to ensure that the efforts of these companies would be coordinated. And if anything went wrong, hopefully I could contact Colonel McNeeley and he would make a decision as to what we should do. For example, if G Company ran into difficulty clearing the beach area and could not turn toward Causeway One early enough, possibly E or F Company could be diverted quickly and seize Causeway One. Well briefly, this was the scheme of maneuver. Now directly in front of Causeway One and Two was Ste.-Marie-du-Monte, which was on a hill kind of overlooking the beaches. And German artillery was known to be in that area.

Having finally gotten on the beach and near the sea wall, I saw a squad of soldiers from G Company depart and I began to follow them. This squad of about six men was being led by a redheaded sergeant whom I recognized from G Company. Unfortunately, I do not recall his name at the present time. As this squad went over the seawall, they began moving toward a wire fence. And I was supposed to follow G Company, I felt it would be appropriate to follow them for awhile so I could determine how much of G Company had gotten inland and turned left down the beach. As this sergeant and his men reached the barbwire fence, the sergeant started through the fence and a tremendous explosion occurred. Obviously, he had hit a mine, stepped on a mine, and all six men fell to the ground, some killed, others wounded. Some of the them were screaming so I ran through them into the area beyond the fence line because my mission was to follow G Company and ensure that Causeway One was secured.

While this was going on, naval gunfire from our battleships, and I recall the name of one was the Black Prince, had lifted from the beach area and was now falling inland. The German artillery from Pointe du Hoc and from the area of Ste.-Marie-du-Mont was coming in and hitting the area which we were located. I began to run over the sand dunes and began receiving small arms fire from obviously some Germans who were dug in on the sand dune line. So periodically I would hit the ground and try to survey the situation and see if I could pick up some of the smoke from the rifle fire of the Germans. I was by myself and did not see anyone. After about two rushes, short rushes from one sand dune to another, I looked around my feet and noted that I was in a minefield. The wind had blown some of the sand around and uncovered some mines. Well, realizing this and looking back towards the beach and having seen the squad of men killed or wounded by the mine, I thought to myself, if I turn around and try to go back to the beach, I'll probably step on a mine. My mission is inland. So, I'm just going to take my chances and continue to move toward the enemy that was firing at me. I got up and made another dash and landed safely. The next time I jumped and ran, the small arms fire from the Germans were cracking around me pretty close, so I made a long leap to a shell hole which I had spied. The shell hole was made by one of our bombs or naval gunfire shells. And while in -mid-air, apparently my right foot caught a tripwire that was attached to a mine. The mine exploded and the force of it slammed me up against the shell hole that I was headed for and numbed my right leg. In fact, I thought I had lost a foot. Looking around very carefully, I finally discovered that I had not been touched, my leg was still intact and after a brief moment of regaining my composure, I decided to continue the advance. By this time, the German rifle fire had subdued a little bit and I assumed that they thought I had been killed by the explosion of the mine.

So, I jumped up quickly and ran directly toward the position I thought these Germans were firing from. Apparently, I startled them somewhat because when I reached the top of the dune line, I saw several individual foxholes. The first one I saw was empty, but hand grenades and rifle ammunition was all around the edge of it. So, I jumped in that fox hole and then quickly determined that this was a rather precarious position to be in because undoubtedly, they had seen me jump in this foxhole. So, I bounced out rather quickly and looked over to my right and within eight yards of me was a German in a foxhole and he had a hand grenade known as the German potato masher, and was in a position to toss it over into the foxhole in which I had been. I turned on the German and shot him at which time Germans started getting up on all sides of me. The total count was nine. They put up their hands, raised their hands very quickly, so I began to corral them in a group.

I noticed that among the captured there was two noncommissioned officers and others appeared to be of lesser rank. I assumed that this was a squad of Germans that I had contacted. I looked over my shoulder toward the channel and the sight I saw just bewildered me. It appeared that the entire channel was choked with ships of all sizes and descriptions. And

I remember thinking at the time that these Germans really had a lot of guts to be shooting small arms fire at even one individual when they had, spread out before them, a panorama of the largest invasion force that a human being had ever seen, at this stage of the game at least. Well, having these prisoners on my hands, I really did not know what to do with them. However, I began to separate the noncommissioned officers from the other soldiers, because that's what we had been trained to do.

Having done this, I turned to my right to survey the surrounding terrain and saw one soldier who had a cloth wrapped around his hand. And obviously he had been hit in the hand. And he was approximately a hundred yards away. So, I called him to come where I was located. When he arrived, it turned out to be a Corporal West from G Company. I asked Corporal West where was the rest of G Company. And he said that they had run into a minefield and were, more or less, to my right rear. I had assumed that G Company was in front of me. Seeing that Corporal West was wounded, I told him to take charge of these prisoners and take them back along the route which he had walked because if he went straight toward the beach, he would have to pass through the minefield that I had just negotiated. So, he took the prisoners and began at a slight angle inland, then would turn, make a semicircle around this minefield and reach the beach. Having accomplished this, I decided to continue moving inland because eventually, G Company would get around the minefield and would be coming down to the beach so I would undoubtedly be able to contact them in that I had taken a short cut, precarious as it might have been. Well, I continued inland and bearing left so that I would be in line with the approach of G Company. Having gone about 300 yards, I saw two enlisted men. I called to them. We got together. I recognized one as being a soldier by the name of Ballard from G Company who was a Browning automatic rifleman and a very excellent shot. The other soldier I did not know, but we teamed up as a group of three.

And I, having seen a large pillbox further down the beach, decided that we should check that pill box out to see if there were any German troops in it, because this pillbox was in the path of which G Company was supposed to follow in order to clean up pillboxes and any enemy parallel to the beach on their way to Causeway One. As we began moving cautiously toward this tremendous pillbox, a German machine-gun pinned us down temporarily, the fire was coming from this pillbox. Fortunately, there was a rather deep ditch close by, so the three of us dived into the ditch and began crawling down the ditch toward the pill box. As we got within, I'd estimate, a hundred and fifty yards of the pillbox, and knowing Ballard was a very good shot with the BAR. While we were in England, I remember we were out doing some firing and a big jackrabbit ran in front of us who were shooting at some stationary targets, and Ballard armed with the BAR, turned that rabbit over in full flight. So, that's the reason I knew that he was an excellent shot with the BAR. I asked Ballard to get a position from the edge of the ditch so he could shoot at this, the embrasures of the pillbox, to determine whether these Germans inside the pillbox really meant business or not, which he did. And his fire was very accurate.

And he let them have several bursts from his BAR and then ducked back down into the ditch, at which time two embrasures of the pillbox began chattering and delivering very accurate and withering machine-gun fire right over the top of our heads. So, we received our answer rather quickly, that this was a formidable pillbox and the occupants really meant business. Accordingly, I turned to the other soldier and asked him if he remembered the route he had taken to get where we were from the beach. He assured me that he knew, so I told him to go back to the beach by following the route which he had just taken and see if he could contact one of the DD tanks (Duplex drive tank) and some other personnel. He was to lead the tank and anybody he could round up and bring them to this position so the tank could deliver fire against the pillbox because we knew that BAR machine-gun fire against the pillbox would be most ineffective.

The soldier took off while Ballard and I continued down the ditch to try and determine if additional enemy or more pillboxes were down the beach line. After passing this pillbox that we were so concerned about, we saw another pillbox much further down the beach, but it was so far that I determined it would be best to wait awhile until this big pillbox was eliminated before proceeding further. Fortunately, we did not have to wait long because the soldier whom I had sent back to the beach to try and secure a tank with some additional personnel must have met some tanks which had landed and were proceeding inland. Two DD tanks approached and the soldier pointed out the target and they began to fire on the pillboxes. The pillbox returned fire momentarily until one of the tanks got a round right in one of the embrasures of the pillbox, at which time a white flag on a pole was run up by the occupants of the pillbox. The Germans then began to come out of the pillbox. Ballard and I, who were very close by this time, in the ditch, counted 36 Germans. Apparently, all the Germans in the area sought cover in this particular pillbox, except the squad that I had run into on the dune line within close proximity of the pillbox. Seeing this, I directed Ballard to keep the Germans covered with his BAR.

And I found another enlisted man who had come up with the DD tanks and he was also from G Company. And we proceeded down the ditch which Ballard and I had previously crawled down for some distance. My objective in doing this was to reach Causeway One as quickly as possible to preclude the Germans from blowing the bridge on the causeway. The enlisted man and I crawled down this ditch as far as we could go. The ditch that we were crawling down was parallel to a dirt road and I assumed that this dirt road was one that would lead us to Causeway One because I knew the map very well but the ditch ran out. So, I told the enlisted man that I was going to dash across the road because there was a hedgerow that ran in what I thought was the direction of Causeway. When I dashed across the road, no one shot at me so I sought a little cover in a small ditch and surveyed the situation. The hedgerow appeared to be perfect for cover and concealment to further approach the causeway. However, I noted the field which we would have to cross to get to the hedgerow and to go through parallel to the hedgerow. It had barbwire stretched around it showing it as German mine-fields. I immediately looked at posts which supported the barbwire because I remembered having been given a piece of intelligence gathered by our intelligence agencies to the effect that if a piece of wire extended directly skyward from the top of the post and that piece of wire was straight, that would indicate the dummy minefield. If, on the other hand, the piece of wire extending skyward from the post was curled like a corkscrew, that was a real minefield. I noted that the wire extending skyward from the post on this minefield was straight, and I began to wonder if the intelligence that we had received in reference to this marking system was accurate or not.

I called the enlisted man to come across the road, which he did, and I explained this to him and told him that the only way I knew to test this bit of intelligence was to get out in the minefield and walk along parallel to the hedgerow and hopefully it would turn out to be a dummy minefield. He was a little reluctant to do this, so I told him to remain where he was and if I stepped on a mine, for him to take off back the route he had followed and contact other people as they came forward. So, I crawled through the wire fence and, talking about walking on eggshells, I was really tiptoeing. I must admit I was somewhat nervous and concerned, but having gotten into the would-be minefield about 10 yards, I detected no bumps in the ground any disturbance of the earth, either old or fresh, so I felt sure that this was a dummy minefield. I then waived to the enlisted man who came forward and we started creeping down the hedgerow. Finally, I peeped over the hedgerow and I could see causeway number one, which was about 150 yards away from us. At about the same time, there was some rifle fire going on across the inundated area on the other side of the causeway bridge. We continued down the hedgerow until we approached within 45 yards of the causeway. And in order to get closer, we'd have to go over the hedgerow and get into a small ditch that was parallel to this dirt road which crossed the causeway. Well, I decided to do this and told the enlisted man to stay on this side of the hedgerow until I got into the ditch and if I didn't get pinned down or anything, then I would wave him forward, which I did. And fortunately, I got within about 30 yards of the causeway itself.

The rifle fire on the other side of the bridge continued sporadically. About this time, two Germans started running down the road toward the causeway from the little village of Pouppeville. And the enlisted man and I saw them at the same time. So, I told the enlisted man to wait. Don't shoot until they got very close to the bridge because I want to be able to eliminate them quickly and not be subjected to any fire. We waited and they approached within 10 yards of the far side of the bridge and I said, "Now!" So, we shot and knocked both of them down.

At this time, we noted some, about a squad of seven or eight Germans who apparently had been coming behind these two Germans, stopped and turned to their right and they got into a skirmish formation and began to move toward the bridge in short rushes. It was easily discernible that they had seen what happened to the two Germans who had run down toward the bridge and they knew that some American forces of some type were near the bridge. So, it appeared to me that they were going to try to outflank the enlisted man and myself. We began shooting at this squad. And about this time, the rile fire on the other side of the inundated area began to pickup intensity. And it appeared to me some were shooting the same members of this squad that the enlisted man and I were shooting at. But then, there was some rifle fire being delivered in our direction. Some of the firing sounded like the M-1 rifle rather than a German rifle. Now I might pause here to mention that before the invasion, all airborne troops and the seaborne troops had been issued a small square of orange cloth as a means of a recognition signal, that if you had come under fire from friendly forces, either from the airborne or the seaborne elements, you were supposed to wave this orange piece of cloth to signify that you were an American or members of the U.S. armed forces. So, I dragged out my square orange cloth, put it on a stick quickly and held it up and in the air and waived it. A few more rifle bullets cracked around. But it wasn't long before I saw and orange flag being waived from our right front, which was the element that I was really concerned about. So, I and the enlisted man breathed a sigh of relief because we felt sure that these were the elements of supposedly the 101st Airborne Division.

Now at this time, the rifle fire was all concentrated towards the squad of Germans who had begun to try to outflank us. Pretty soon, the German squad did not fire any more. Within about 15 minutes this all transpired, so I told the enlisted man that I was going to run across the bridge, get on the other side to be sure that we held that bridge, and if I didn't get into any trouble, that I would wave him forward. So, he covered me and I jumped up and dashed across the bridge. As I was running across the bridge, I glanced down and saw a tremendous bomb had been, it looked like an air force type bomb, had been placed in the bridge and had been wired for detonation. And it just flashed through my mind that probably the two Germans that the enlisted man and I had eliminated or knocked down, they were coming to explode the bomb and thus destroy the bridge. The two Germans were lying on the ground, that the enlisted man and I had shot, and several Germans were lying on the right and left side of this road, some in the bushes, some in a slight ditch and some were just along the edge of the road. So, as I ran by, I noticed one who appeared to be shaking a bit. So, I just took my right foot and kicked him in the thigh. And at that time, he jumped up, held up his hands and surrendered and then the Germans began to stand up all around me, both sides of the road. I got them out in the middle of the road and about that time, I looked up the road toward Pouppeville and an American soldier jumped over the hedgerow, with his rifle at the ready. So, I hollered to him, "Don't shoot," because I had some prisoners. I marched these prisoners on up to where he was, and he turned out to be a member of the 101st Airborne Division.

So, we shook hands and he stated that General Taylor, Maxwell Talor, the Commanding General of the 101st Airborne Division, was just across the hedgerow. Before we could do anything, a couple more enlisted men came over the hedgerow and then General Taylor. So, I greeted General Taylor, saluted and shook hands with him and I remember immediately after shaking hands with him, I looked at my watch and it was 11:05, June 6th. The reason I mention the time and this incident in particular is, as far as I know, this constituted the first official contact made between the airborne and the seaborne forces. After talking to General Taylor, General Gavin, Assistant Division Commander of the 82nd Airborne Division, appeared, and it was quite obvious at that point that the 101st and 82nd airborne divisions had missed their drop zone, so to speak, and were more or less intermingled, the 101st and 82nd. I told General Taylor the scheme of maneuvers of the Second Battalion and told him that I expected E and F and G Company would be coming across this causeway fairy quickly if they had not run into too much difficulty on this strip of land between the beach and the inundated area. And he indicated to me that he was headed for Ste.-Mere-Eglise because that was where he was supposed to have landed when he deboosed from the airplane. I recommended that he remain where he was and pretty soon, our battalion would be coming through there and we would provide him some protection. He could then follow us as far as we were going that afternoon, and that we were going to bypass Ste.-Mere-Eglise. So, we'd be right of Ste.-Mere-Eglise but at least we could get him closer to Ste.-Mere-Eglise and then he, on his own, if he wanted to, could proceed to Ste.-Mere-Eglise.

Having done that, I ran back down to the road, crossed the causeway again, took a closer look at this bomb that was in the causeway and went down a little further so I could catch any members of E, F and G Company that might be moving in my direction and direct them to Causeway One. And it wasn't long before elements of E Company who, having hit the inundated area, turned to their left as they were supposed to and began sweeping the area down to Causeway One. They encountered some enemy, but not nearly as many as we had anticipated. Pretty soon, elements of F Company began to arrive, so E Company led off, followed by elements of G Company and, I'd say within 20 minutes elements of G Company who had begun sweeping the beach area began to arrive. So, it wasn't long until we had a sizeable element of the battalion assembled and moving toward Ste.-Maria-du-Mont and Ste.-Mere-Eglise being to the left.

Eventually, Colonel McNeeley, the battalion commander, arrived and the battalion was moving. It wasn't long after that that Colonel James A. Van Fleet the regimental commander, arrived. He had come down behind the Second Battalion. When I saw Colonel Van Fleet, I told him I had seen General Taylor and had recommended to General Taylor that he tag on to the tail of the battalion and go as far as he could with us in his effort to get to Ste.-Mere-Eglise. Colonel Van Fleet thanked me and proceeded back down towards the tail end of the battalion in hopes of contacting General Taylor. I might pause here to mention that later, Colonel Van Fleet was never able to contact General Taylor because General Taylor decided not to remain with the Second Battalion, the Eighth Regiment. But apparently, he and about fifteen members of the 101st Airborne Division and maybe some of the 82nd, on their own, began moving towards Ste.-Mere-Eglise. I assumed they made it. I never did take time to check with General Taylor later to see if he got through that afternoon or had to spend the night and eventually got to Ste.-Mere-Eglise.

Having secured assigned Causeway One, Two and Three, and having gotten the battalion back together, so to speak, we proceeded inland toward Ste.-Marie-du-Mont in hopes of contacting the elements of the First Battalion who had landed on our right and had a mission of proceeding toward Ste.-Marie-du-Mont, but passing to the right side of it. We met sporadic resistance in approaching Ste.-Marie-du-Mont, but eventually we got into the little village. There were about three things that impressed me when we got into the village. There was sporadic firing from snipers in buildings in the little village, and once in a while you would hear a round being fired from a muffled position, in other words, the sound of the rifle had a muffled sound to it. This was coming from the town square, where there was a church in the middle of the town square. It had a very tall steeple or spire. I dodged around some buildings, worked my way up to that town square and there, on one side of the street, in fact, there was a vehicle that had come around a corner, a German vehicle. It was a little half track arrangement, opened top half track arrangement, the first one I had ever seen, and in this vehicle were two dead Germans. Now the vehicle, having turned the corner, someone had shot the two Germans and apparently shot the driver first and the vehicle went out of control and was more or less angled across the street and the front end was up on a curb of the street.

Eventually I contacted a member of the 101st Airborne Division and he told me that they had some casualties in the village. And I asked about this rifle that appeared to have been coming from the town square. And he said, "Oh sir, that's the first sergeant. He's up in the church steeple. In fact, he killed these two Germans in this vehicle." Well, in about five or ten minutes, out came this first sergeant, 101st Airborne Division, from the church. And we said a word or two and I commended him on the job that he was doing and told him if there were casualties in the village, to gather them up and hold them in the town square. I said I was positive that medical personnel following the Second Battalion along with the Second battalion could assist in taking care of them and eventually evacuating them.

I proceeded through town about two more blocks and sitting on the base of an old pitcher pump type arrangement (a big handled pump and around the base is a wooden platform where one puts the bucket on to pump the water in), and on that base was sitting an airborne soldier, U.S. airborne soldier. He had been wounded in the face and hand apparently from a rifle grenade and possibly from small arms fire. Someone had wrapped him in bandages. Both hands were wrapped and bloody and his entire face was covered with gauze bandages and it was blood soaked. I spoke to him and he was able to mumble through the gauze that was around his face, all except his nose, and I told him that help would be along very soon. This was a real shocking sight to see a man sitting there with his head bowed over, but sitting upright, and completely wrapped in bandages for every part of the skin one could see. Yet he was conscious and made no complaint.

Having passed through Ste.-Marie-du-Mont, we then began angling somewhat toward Ste.-Mere-Eglise. It wasn't long before we ran into stiff resistance from German troops who were dug in along hedgerows and occupying farm buildings. And if you may recall, in the Normandy area they had huge dairy farms. And around each house were a barn and silos, usually there was a stone wall. In addition, the hedgerows themselves were rather formidable. The hedgerow in Normandy is much different from what we call a hedgerow in the United States. In Normandy, hedgerows were apparently created by farmers when they were picking up rocks out of the field. They would throw them all along on the edge of the field and then, plowing the field, dirt would be banked up on the rocks and throw them on this original rock base. Pretty soon, these hedgerows became rock and dirt that supported trees and bushes. The bases of these hedgerows were anywhere from 8 to 10 feet wide at the bottom and tapered up to about 1 foot, the width at the top. As I say, they supported sizeable trees and underbrush. So, you could take advantage of that for cover and good concealment.

In addition, General Rommel, who had visited the Normandy area a few months prior to the invasion, thought it would be a great idea to put up poles in fields, of any size, to preclude airplanes from landing and gliders from landing and impale paratroopers, when they were dropped from aircraft. And he had put the Germans and the Frenchman to work erecting these poles. And in every field along the coast that would be a potential drop zone for these, hundreds and hundreds of poles would be sticking up. With that, along with the hedgerows and trees on top of the hedgerows, that's a pretty formidable obstacle to gliders and airborne troops landing. And I do not recall us ever receiving any briefing by our intelligence agencies that mentioned the hedgerows or mentioned the formidable obstacles that the trees and underbrush on these hedgerows would have, referenced airborne and glider landing troops and the restrictions that would be placed on any type vehicle, full tracked or wheeled vehicles. I do remember a little bit of information that was given to us about some poles having been erected in fields after General Rommel's visit, but nothing was ever said, to the best of my knowledge, about the hedgerows.

And that connection, we soon learned, that due to the checkerboard fashion of the fields, each surrounded by a hedgerow, we soon learned a tactic that the Germans were utilizing. For example, we would run into a German prepared position. So, the riflemen would lean up against the hedgerow and start shooting at the Germans in their positions. And the machine guns were normally taken down a hedgerow and put in position on top of a hedgerow, hoping to get enfilade fire into the German position. In other words, flanking fire into the German position. Well this was all well and good, but pretty soon, what the Germans would do is they would hold their machine guns in reserve and once we got our machine guns in position, they would run down a hedgerow and turn a corner and run into another field and find a good machine-gun position that would give us flanking fire, take their machine-gun off the hedgerow where it had been firing initially and then put an automatic firing weapon in that position and run their machine gun down to the position they had selected to give us enfilade fire. And here we'd be shooting with our machine gun. We would be shooting at what once was the German machine gun position and now, an automatic rifle position. And we'd be chattering away at each other, and all of a sudden, from your right flank would come immediately, by surprise, the machine gun fire from a German machine gun. Now we wondered where in the world they were getting all these machine guns from. Well, it didn't take long to figure out what they were doing. So, we employed a similar tactic. We'd set up our machine guns, fire a while and then a German would run down the hedgerow, turn a corner, start firing enfilade fire on us, we'd pull our machine gun down, put a BAR man in that position, and then take our machine gun and run it down, turn a couple corners and put it up on the hedgerow and give flanking fire to the enemy position. So, this is the way it happened quite often.

Well, now back to our continued advance toward Ste.-Mere-Eglise. Having run into the German resistance, we were fighting and inching our way forward and eventually learned that there were American troops, airborne troops, in Ste.-Mere-Eglise, that were holding the town of Ste.-Mere-Eglise. We were trying to reach them on D-Day, but having run into this stiff opposition, we didn't know whether we could do so or not. So, we were fighting very hard to break through this band of enemy that were between us and Ste.-Mere-Eglise. It was getting late in the afternoon. And rumor was passed that German tanks had been sighted to our immediate front and for everyone to anticipate an attack by German tanks. Well, we had to make a decision as to how long we should continue to fight and to try to move forward to get as much maneuver room as possible from the inundated areas so we would not have our backs to the inundated area. At the same time we had to prepare for a counterattack by large numbers of tanks and/or German infantry. Colonel McNeeley and I discussed this at length and decided to continue to press forward in order to get as much maneuver room as we possibly could. And this we did, and continued to fight until almost dark. And, as you may know, that time of the year, the sun stays up for a long time and daylight prevails until 11:30 at night. Eventually, we decided we better hold up because everyone should have an opportunity to dig in very good to withstand a potential counterattack. And it appeared logical to us that if the Germans were going to counterattack in force, this would be the most opportune time to counterattack us as quickly as possible to stop us and chew us up, so to speak, and run us back into the channel, if at all possible, before we could get more troops ashore and enlarge the beachhead. So, everyone began to dig in behind hedgerows and putting in anti-tank weapons and setting out mines to withstand this German counterattack, as we felt sure would occur.

Fortunately for us, it did not occur. You can speculate what determined the Germans not attacking. One reason was, as I recall, Hitler did not want to, he did not think this was the main invasion force and he was holding his armored divisions in reserve to wait and really counterattack the main thrust which he thought was coming across the channel in the Dover area. In addition, our air force was quite active in the air further beyond where we could see and caught some German convoys on the road as well as some tanks, which crippled them. And I'll tell you a little more about one convoy I saw near Ste.-Mere-Eglise that had been pretty well riddled by our air force.

Having decided and received confirmation from the regimental head-quarters that we should button up, so to speak, for the night. And this was around ten o'clock, I'd estimate 10:00 p.m. The companies of the battalion began to dig in or select positions to dig in. And I, being the S-3 of the battalion, went to each company to be sure that we had the best positions possible to counter any counterattack the Germans may throw at us, and being positively sure that each company, each of the companies were tied in with each other on their right and left flanks respectively. It was in the wee hours of the morning by the time I could accomplish all this and get back to below battalion CP, the command post, which was cut in behind a hedgerow, on the corner of a hedgerow. Having assured Colonel McNeeley that everything was set up and having eaten a K ration, I tried to get a few winks of sleep. Well, the artillery was firing all night long, both going out and coming in and trying to get ready for the next morning attack. We were going to jump off at just before daylight. So, we had very little time for any relaxation or sleep. The next morning, we jumped off at first light, moving toward Ste.-Mere-Eglise. Now we knew that on D plus one, some gliders were to come in, reinforcing elements of the airborne divisions.

So, we began to press hard in the attack the morning of D plus one and it was getting along fairly well until we ran into a complex of dairy farms where each of them was separated by a road and maybe a few hundred yards. But each had a big stone wall around its respective complex, such as a house, stone house, and barns and silos and other small buildings. The Germans were using these buildings and stone walls for defense purposes. So, we began attacking two of these complexes at the same time. And I recall being on the left side of the road that separated two of these large complexes. And we were getting a terrific amount of small arms fire from these areas. And I was near...F Company, on the left. E Company was across the road. And we were shooting mortars at these houses and artillery had been brought in. And we were inching forward.

And I crawled up behind a hedgerow, where some of the F Company's men were, and very close to me was Mickey Donahue, the tremendous boxer that I coached and really, I didn't coach him much. He knew much more than I did about boxing. But anyway, I highly respected old Mickey. And I crawled up on top of this hedgerow and was peeping over it and I saw a German run down the hedgerow on the other side of the field. So, I shot at him and a couple of other people shot and he went down. About this time, ...a tremendous explosion occurred very close to Mickey Donahue. And I looked, when it exploded, I glanced to my right and I saw a German's arm come down, and I figured right quick what had happened. He, the German, had thrown a potato masher hand grenade and looped it up in the air and what I saw was his arm coming down right after having hurled the hand grenade. So, I waited a while and the German stuck his head up and I took a crack at him and I never heard from him again. But the mortar rounds began to come in. In that this first explosion occurred pretty close to Mickey, I crawled back down the other side of the hedgerow and crawled down to where Mickey was and he had been hit. He was bleeding from the mouth and he really looked like he was going to die pretty soon. So, I dragged him up in the little road and turned him over on his back, put his helmet under his head, took out his canteen and put the canteen down by his body, by his right hand. And a couple of other enlisted men were there. I told them to move on, that we had called for the medics and we hollered for medical personnel. About this time, elements of the company began to move because it appeared that we had crushed the opposition immediately to our front. So, I had to abandon Mickey, and I moved on with the company.

We got up near one of these houses and three Germans came running around a stone wall. Well, I hollered, "Halt!" And they threw up their hands. And I made them lie down on the ground because I knew if they stood up, somebody seeing a German uniform would let them have a blast. So, they laid down on the ground and I ran on and told them to stay there. When I ran into this courtyard, inside the stone wall, I noticed there was a Frenchman standing in the front door and he was making all kinds of signs with his hand so I ran up there to the door and he indicated that somebody inside the house had been wounded. So, I ran in. A couple of enlisted men came in behind me. And there was a middle-aged woman and a small boy, I'd say around 10 years old, and this man. The woman had been hit in the stomach, somewhere in the abdomen, by a mortar shell or artillery shell fragment and she was bleeding profusely. And the little boy was sitting in a chair just looking, with a stare in his eye. Obviously, it was his mother who was wounded. She was making no noise other than breathing heavily. And the Frenchman, he was quite excited so I calmed him down and told him that we'd get him a medical person there to assist his wife and he thanked me. So, I ran on. I checked later and they assured me that this lady was taken care of and she lived. And neither the young boy nor the man was hit. On the German soldiers that I had told to lie down on the ground, I ran back by there on the way later, on my way over to check with the left flank of E Company, and one of the German soldiers had been killed. The other two were not there, so they had been taken prisoner. I don't know how the one was killed. It could have been an accident or it could have been a mortar round hit them. I did not check him to determine whether rifle fire or shrapnel or hand grenade had killed him. But of the three, only one had been killed and the other two obviously had been taken prisoner.

Having passed these two formidable defensive positions, we began to have a little more success. About this time, I estimate around 9 o'clock in the morning, maybe a little earlier, some gliders began to come in and the gliders would circle over us and receive no enemy fire. And then, they'd pass over this band of enemy between us and Ste.-Mere-Eglise and get all kinds of fire. Then they'd go over Ste.-Mere-Eglise and receive no fire. And I can imagine those pilots on the gliders were most confused because, you can imagine the confusion if you fly over one part, you'd get no fire. Fly over another, you'd get enemy fire. Go over another, you'd get nothing. And then make a circle, and the same thing would occur all over again. Well, some of the gliders were coming in and crashing against the poles that had been erected in these fields. Some were hitting the trees on hedgerows. But eventually, one landed in the field next to where I was standing at the time.

And as soon as it touched ground, the crew jumped out and ran around and opened the thing up and dragged out a French 75 gun. And they began to load that thing and start shooting. Well, they were shooting back toward the beach. Well, I hollered as loud as I could and finally got one of their attention and waved the orange piece of cloth I had, and ran over there and told them, "Stop firing!" Your firing in the wrong direction! You're firing at the beach." Well, this officer in charge says, "Well, I am sorry but we are really confused." And I thought to myself anyone would be confused in a situation like this. The experiences that they had, flying over and no one shooting at them and then, over in another area in close proximity, everybody shoots at them. Go a little further and no one shoots. Then you make a circle and the same thing occurs. So, he thanked me and I said, "Well, I'm just glad that you didn't shoot me when I was running across the field because I hoped you saw this orange flag." He said, "I saw that," and again, I was thankful for having the small orange flag as a recognition signal.

As we pushed on towards the Ste.-Mere-Eglise that day, we ran into sporadic resistance until we got within, I'd estimate a thousand yards, maybe a little further, from Ste.-Mere-Eglise. And again, we ran into a very formidable defense. We knew that the Third Battalion of the Eight Regiment, having landed after the First and Second Battalion, had come ashore and now were on our left flank. So, we began to receive quite a bit of fire from our left flank. So, we halted temporarily and I talked to Colonel McNeeley. I suggested that we should try to contact the Third battalion because it appeared to me that they were much further behind us than had been reported. We were unable to contact the Third Battalion by radio, so I took two enlisted men and told Colonel McNeeley that I was going to go to the left and see if I could not contact the Third Battalion.

We started out and came to a dirt road, started up the dirt road and we saw many German vehicles parked on a macadam road (broken stone) that was leading into Ste.-Mere-Eglise. We approached those vehicles very cautiously, and I saw a couple of Germans run down the side of the road to our left and then disappear. Well, I told these two enlisted men that we would ease up to these trucks to determine whether there's any additional personnel around them. As we were approaching the trucks, I saw an airborne trooper, U.S. airborne trooper, hanging on his chute, was hanging on a telephone line or power line and his feet were about a foot off the ground. And his throat had been cut. Well, this angered us. And the two enlisted men began to make some threatening comments, and I told them that, now look, we'll never do anything like that because this is what we're fighting against. We later saw a couple more paratroopers, U.S. paratroopers who had been killed while hanging in trees. We went back to the German trucks. I inspected several of them carefully. There must have been 25 or 30 of them lined up on this macadam road. And they had been strafed by the U.S. Air Force. All trucks had been knocked out. One or two had burned, but the majority were just riddled with 50 caliber machine gun bullets. Having seen the direction that these three or four German soldiers had run, I decided to follow this macadam road a little further down to the left to see if we could not contact the Third Battalion.

We sneaked down in that direction quite a distance, saw nothing and it occurred to me that maybe I was over into the Third Battalion's area, area of responsibility. But about this time, we spied a group of houses which was on the other side of this paved road. And there was, it looked like a deep ditch that ran down close to these houses. And we heard rifle firing coming from that direction. So, I thought, well, the Third Battalion must be further to the left than we anticipated and they are now attacking this group of houses. So, we went further down this highway and got over in this big ditch that I was talking about. And crawling down this ditch, and about that time, we noticed some Germans were in the house directly in front of us and some were looking out of the second story windows, some were peeping around the corner of a building on the ground floor, so I told the enlisted men we were going down and take them under fire and hopefully help out the Third Battalion.

So, we sneaked down a little further and got good positions near where the hedgerow turned. And we lined up on the hedgerow. And I told them I'd take the man who was in one window on the ground floor. The soldier on my left, was to take the one who was peeping around the corner of the building and there was about two or three standing to the right of the building, so I told the man on my right to take them under fire. And we shot simultaneously and a couple of them hit the ground. The one that I shot, he disappeared and I don't know whether he fell or what. At that time, the German on the top floor stuck his head out of a window, the top floor window, so, I shat at him and he disappeared, but another soldier appeared and stuck his rifle out of the window and was kind of surveying the situation trying to determine where the fire was coming from. So, I shot him and he fell back into the window, into the room. Now, the point here is that when you're shooting out of a window, never get right up to the window and poke the rifle barrel out of the window. The best thing to do is to step back a few yards and shoot through the window, and you would not be exposed to persons looking in the window from the outside. Well, we continued to shoot at these personnel who were returning fire. They couldn't see us, but they were shooting in our direction, the bullets were cracking around but were not coming too close to us.

About this time, a few rounds of artillery began to land close to this house and some houses to the left of us. And I determined it must be a crossroad up there, more or less a little group of houses constituting a village. Well, I didn't like the sound of this artillery, because it sounded like it was coming from the beach area and therefore, that artillery was supporting the Third Battalion. So, I told these enlisted men we'd better turn around and go back up this ditch and try to get back to our area because I felt we were too far over into Third Battalion area and the Third Battalion was way behind us. So, we were way out in front of the Third Battalion and they could be concentrating the artillery fire in the positions we had been attacking from the flank.

Just as we started back up this ditch, the U.S. artillery started coming in and I have never in my life felt like that before or since. The artillery was massed artillery. I don't know how many battalions but when they turned loose, the shells coming through the air sounded like a flock of ducks and the rounds began to hit all around us. We began running back up the ditch, and a dog came running from this village and started to jump over the ditch and the artillery cut him in half right over us. A round came down into the ditch and hit in a big puddle of water and covered us with mud from head to foot. Well, seeing this, I told these enlisted me that we were going to get out of this artillery as quickly as possible. And we were not going back up that ditch. We'd jump up and run across an open field to our right and go back toward the Second Battalion. I said, "On my command of three, let's take off." So, the artillery was coming in, I just can't describe it. It was just a b-b-b-r-r-r-r-VOOM! So, when I counted three, we jumped up and started running across this open field. Nobody shot at us because they were trying to take cover, like we were, from this artillery. We ran as far as we could until we just gave out, and fell down right in the middle of this open field and the artillery was falling behind us where we had been in this ditch. I looked over my left shoulder and saw the trees crumbling and the dirt being dug up in the ditch we had been in and I said, "Let's go," and we ran again. We hit the ground one more time and on the third rush, we were able to get out of the artillery concentration, but we were covered from head to toe in mud and dirt. When we finally got back to the battalion, the first thing I said to Colonel McNeeley, and I was still shaking, visibly shaking, I told him that we had inadvertently got into our own artillery fire and I never want an experience like that again. I told him the full story and we were finally able to recontact the Third Battalion by radio and determined that what I had surmised was correct, that they had massed their artillery, mortars and everything else in a preparation for an attack against this village. The crossroad that I had mentioned earlier was the registering point. So, everything was being concentrated right in that area where we had been. There is one more comment. I have studiously avoided ever getting into anybody else's area of responsibility without notifying them ahead of time, because the way the U.S. was able to mass its artillery fire was a wonder of the world and still is a technique that other armies are trying to emulate.

Having talked to Colonel McNeeley and told him about what we had seen in reference to some of our parachutists having been killed while hanging in their chutes in trees and power lines, he mentioned to me that he had seem some of the same and other personnel of the battalion had seen similar incidences. I recommended to him that we pass the word to the company commanders to inform all officers, all noncommissioned officers and down to the enlisted man that we did not condone such barbaric behavior and members of the Second Battalion would not take out their frustrations and anger against any German prisoners. And if we caught this being done, the individuals would be subjected to a general court martial. Colonel McNeeley agreed and this word was passed to every individual in the battalion, just to preclude any reprisals against what we had seen the Germans were capable of doing. And I think it was a wise decision because something like this can get out of hand and a unit could be ruined and it's just an inhumane treatment of prisoners. It is against the Geneva Convention and the rationale of sound, sane human beings.

Earlier, I mentioned having put Mickey Donahue in a road and putting his helmet under his head and really, I thought he would die. A couple of years after World War Two ended, one day I was talking with a nurse who was a first cousin of my college roommate. Her name was Jenny Dubose the cousin of Richard Dubose with whom I roomed for four years at Presbyterian College. And she asked me if I had ever known a soldier by the name of Donahue. I told her, well, the only Donahue I could think of was a fellow by the name of Mickey Donahue, but I was sure that he had died. She said, "Oh no, he's the one I'm talking about and he's in Valley Forge General Hospital where I am a nurse and he is still alive, but paralyzed from his waist down. This was a very pleasant shock to me, that he was still alive. So, I contacted him and we corresponded for quite a while. And then, as things do happen, I lost contact with him for several years because of my overseas duties and the Korean war, followed by the Vietnam War. But in July 1978, while attending a meeting of the Fourth Infantry Division National Association meeting in Clearwater, Florida, a friend of Mickey's arranged for me to talk with Mickey on the telephone as well as arrangements for now retired full general Van Fleet to speak with Mickey. So, we were able to talk to Mickey and had a grand old-time reestablishing contact with him.

Back to D-Day, we were approaching Ste.-Mere-Eglise. The Third Battalion, having made their organized attack against the crossroad and village I was talking about earlier, we then joined hands, so to speak, and pressed on towards Ste.-Mere-Eglise. We were eventually able to eliminate the final resistance between us and the airborne troops, members of the 82nd Airborne Division, who were holding Ste.-Mere-Eglise. It was late in the afternoon, and as we came in to Ste.-Mere-Eglise, we began to take up positions on the left side of Ste.-Mere-Eglise. I contacted Colonel McNeeley and told him that I was going to go down to the right to see if I could contact the commander of the airborne forces in Ste.-Mere-Eglise to get a better tie in with him, which I did. And I asked several soldiers where the commander was, and learned his name was Lieutenant Colonel Vandervoort, who was commanding a battalion of the 82nd Airborne Troops who were in Ste.-Mere-Eglise.

I finally located Colonel Vandervoort and to my surprise, he was sitting in a wheelbarrow and obviously he had been wounded in the leg. An enlisted man was pushing him around in the wheelbarrow. And he was still in command even though he had been wounded. We talked for a few minutes and I asked Colonel Vandervoort how his troops were disposed. Having learned of this, I asked him if he had a fairly secure position. He said his position was very tenuous and he was afraid that the Germans were massing for a counterattack. I explained to him and showed him on a map where the Second Battalion, Eight Regiment was located and he requested that we move forward and secure his left flank, that no one was on his left flank because most of his troops were to the right and right center of the position we were located at the time. I assured him that we would do so and as an afterthought, he told me where he anticipated the counterattack would come from. So, I told him that what we might do is, once we got into position, that we would make a limited attack and flanking attack and try to thwart any counterattack, in that we had just moved into position and I felt the Germans would be surprised if another Battalion were to attack, they would not know we were there, we might be able to catch them at a disadvantage. He thought that this was a great idea, so I left in haste and reported to Colonel McNeeley.

Colonel McNeeley ordered that the Battalion be immediately moved forward and once contact between all companies had been established, to let him know. We did this and as luck would have it, about the time we got completely coordinated, the Germans did launch a counterattack against Ste.-Mere-Eglise. And the main thrust was head-on, so to speak, toward the battalion of the 82nd Airborne Division while we were extended to the left flank. Realizing this, Colonel McNeeley directed that we, the Second Battalion, conduct a flanking attack and more or less swing around from left to right and sweep toward the front of the 82nd's battalion. We began doing this and eventually began going parallel to a sunken road. Now a sunken road in Normandy is a road that has been worn down by travel and hedgerows on both sides so it obscures one's vision of anybody running up and down this road. The German counterattack came across a wide-open field and they were trying to get in this sunken road to get a better position from which to launch a close-in, vigorous attack against the airborne troops. As luck would have it, when we executed the flanking movement, we caught these Germans coming across the open field and began to shoot them down in the field. Well, the Germans, realizing this, came running across the field and gotten into this sunken road. The Second Battalion continued to sweep down that road and I hate to describe the situation, but German bodies were stacked up in that sunken road, a sight that one would hardly believe. To give you an illustration, once we reached the point where we had anticipated stopping the attack, we did and then pulled back and began to dig holes protective shelters in the sunken road to button up for the night. Actually, the troops of the Second Battalion had to stack German bodies two and three deep in this sunken road in order to dig a foxhole. To further support this, the following morning, five Germans, live Germans gave themselves up by punching U.S. enlisted soldiers at daylight the next morning, indicating to them that they would like to be taken prisoners. These live soldiers were mixed in with the dead soldiers. They feinted being dead and stayed there all night....

Northern France Campaign

The 4th Division would continue pursuing the Germans over the next several months. On June 25, 1944, the Division took part in the capture of Cherbourg on the Cotentin Peninsula. And on July 6 – 12, 1944, the Division fought near Periers and broke through the left flank of the German Seventh Army, stemming the German drive forward toward Avranches. In August 1944, the Division moved to Paris and assisted the French in the liberation of their capital.

Entering Germany –
Attacking the Siegfried Line

On September 14, 1944, the 4th Division attacked the Siegfried Line at Schnee Eifel after moving into Belgium through Houffalize. Soon, the 8th Infantry Regiment marched into the Hurtgen Forest battle.

The Hurtgen Forest

On November 6, 1944, the 4th Division reached the Hurtgen Forest, where a lengthy battle took place, that lasted until early December. In its one month of fighting in the Hurtgen Forest, the 4th Infantry Division suffered 4,053 battle casualties and more than 2,000 non-battle casualties. Brave men fought side by side. Many died on the battlefield and many would come home forever changed. Four Ivy 4th Division Soldiers received the Medal of Honor for their actions above and beyond the call of duty during the Battle of the Hurtgen Forest - Lt. Col. George Mabry, Jr.; 1st Lt. Bernard Ray; and Pfc. Marcario Garcia and Private Pedro Cano.

Captain John C. Swearingen of the 2nd Battalion, 8th Infantry described the first phase of Mabry's Medal of Honor actions:

"The men of Company G were pinned down before a minefield and they were quite shaken. They had fought their way steadily forward for several days under deadly fire. They couldn't find a way through the minefield and 15 casualties were in the field before them. Shells and mortars were falling among them and some were bursting in the trees above them. Colonel Mabry helped dress some of the wounded, then entered the minefield alone and picked his way through. When the men followed, he recognized their units and set out alone to contact Company E, on our flank. Going to them he was exposed to rifle and machine gun fire from the enemy. Fire had been coming from a bunker ahead and he charged this position, but found it had been deserted, and rushed a second bunker. As he approached nine Germans ran out to meet him. Using the butt of his rifle he smashed the head of the first German who approached him. He used a straight butt stroke. He bayoneted a second who came through the middle of the group of Krauts."

Captain George K. Devine who commanded Company G that day picked up the narrative: "Colonel Mabry never hesitated charging into the nine Germans. After he had bayoneted and slugged the first two, the remaining seven Germans ganged around him and it was a melee when some of my boys came along and waded into the fight. That settled it and the Germans withdrew as the battalion moved into the hill position."

Battle of the Bulge

Having been grounded down rather severely in the Hurtgen Forest, the 4th Division was sent to the "quiet sector" near Luxembourg to regroup and lick our wounds. As I recall the division was deployed on about a 30-mile front. My Battalion had been reduced in strength to a point where my Companies consisted of not more than 40 men each. Further, my Battalion had been placed in Division Reserve (first and only time this happened during WWII).

Due to my lack of troop strength I began reorganizing the Battalion from Squad level on up in anticipation of eventually receiving replacements. Accordingly, we did some firing of weapons, small unit tactical training and motor maintenance for a few days. In that my Battalion was the Division Reserve, I decided we had better practice some Company march discipline so that we could move quickly and effectively if called upon. On that day, while we were engaged in this exercise, I received a radio message to report to Division Headquarters immediately. Therefore, I took off (it was about 1100 hours) in a jeep with driver and radio operator only.

Upon reaching the Division Command Post, I was rushed in to see General Raymond O. Barton, The Division Commanding General. He was pacing the floor, chain smoking and appeared quite disturbed. He asked me if I knew what was going on. I said, "No sir", to which he said the Germans had launched a major counterattack and were pouring through the Divisional position which was spread over a 30-mile sector. He did not know where the Germans were or in what force. He had also lost contact with many elements of the Division. He then took me over to a map, put his arms around my shoulders and made the following points. (One) – My Battalion was the only Reserve the Division had. He was rounding up every available man at Division headquarters, to reconstitute a Division Reserve when he committed my Battalion. He then issued the shortest oral order I ever received. In words to the effect he said, "proceed up this main road (pointing to the map) until you hit the enemy then attack! Once you have done that, I'll try to get these cooks and bakers up to you, if possible. There will be no one on your right or left. You got that?" "Yes sir", I replied. He than asked where my Battalion was and how soon could I get them moving. My reply was, "immediately" because they were already mounted in trucks and practicing motor march procedures. He said, "good, get going!"

I dashed outside and in the clear over the radio informed my Battalion Executive Officer James "Chick" W. Haley to get the entire Battalion on the road, designated a route to take and instructed him to move as fast as possible and that I would intercept the Battalion somewhere along that route. I then jumped into my jeep and took off toward the Echternach area.

After traveling only, a couple miles, we began encountering hundreds of civilians streaming towards Luxembourg. When asked if they had seen any Germans they would only point to their rear and keep moving.

I don't recall how far we traveled under these conditions but it felt like 30 miles. Rather abruptly there were no civilians and the country side was extremely quiet. The paved road took a sharp turn to the left and ran along a high ridge. As we proceeded along this stretch of road, we came under very accurate direct fire from assault guns and artillery. I told the jeep driver to "floor-board" it and we ran the gauntlet and slipped off the road into a field behind a small hill. Now we were faced with the problem of getting back to the paved road on the other end of the ridge and stop the battalion before it could be decimated by the German fire on the ridge. It took quite a while to work the jeep cross country and back to the road, but, as luck would have it, as we reached a point above 100 yards from the road, I spied the Battalion column charging up the road with guidon's flying on the trucks. Accordingly, I was able to turn the Battalion off the road short of the ridge.

As the Companies dismounted, I walked along with each company commander in turn and issued an oral fragmentary order. Basically, the order was to attack in a column of Companies to siege a dominant hill mass that overlooked a "Y" of two paved roads that converged to constitute a main highway leading to Luxembourg. When the lead Company hit the enemy the second Company in line would automatically move to the right or left of the lead Company (dependent on the terrain) and attack immediately. I would be with the 3ʳᵈ Company and employ it accordingly to the situation.

Again, as luck would have it, as we reached a point about 200 yards short of the crest of that dominant hill mass, we had a meeting engagement with the Germans. Fortunately, we attacked vigorously and were able to take the military crest of the hill that positioned us to overlook the "Y" of these roads and command a defile at the junction of the "Y".

We held that position for about 7 days with no contact with any other unit and lost contact with our artillery for about 3 days. Suffered 4 daylight attacks by the Germans. One of the attacks the Germans tried to use tanks but the Defile at Junction of the "Y" was only wide enough to accommodate 1 tank at a time and we mined the Defile. Withstood two German night attacks. The hill was so steep we could hear the Germans climbing up towards us. Therefore, we held our fire until they would get within 15 to 20 yards of our position before opening up with everything we had. One day a Lieutenant from the Reserve Company (E Company) while on patrol killed 3 Germans to our immediate rear. This reassured me the Germans were freely patrolling to my rear and probably knew we were isolated. One day later another patrol ambushed another German patrol and killed 4 Germans and captured an officer (A Lieutenant Colonel I believe) who had a written order. I do not recall what (German) headquarter issued the order but believe it was an Army Group or Division. The order directed the German units to our front to launch an attack two days from that date at 0530 hours: Destroy All Enemy To Their Front And Proceed To Luxembourg At All Cost. I do not recall any words in the order that stated that no prisoners would be taken or that prisoners would be killed. It did state to destroy all enemy to your front and proceed to Luxembourg at all cost.

When this order fell into my hands, I was more concerned about saving our skins more than who issued it, etc. In addition, I wanted the order to get into Intelligence channel's ASAP in the hopes that somebody would send up a unit to help me out a bit. In fact, the Germans opposing us were fairly decent fellows. For example, one morning about 200 civilians came down the left prong of the "Y" trying to get through so they could head towards Luxembourg. At the time we were exchanging small arms fire and motor fire. I directed all fire to cease whereupon the Germans stopped shooting so we permitted the refugees to go through our position and then resumed the fire fight when they had cleared the area.

When I read the German order, I decided something had to be done to throw them off balance. Accordingly, I decided to make a limited attack the next morning before daylight. Therefore, I directed one of the front-line Companies to pull back and join the Reserve Company. The other front-line Company thinned out and occupied some of the fox holes previously occupied by the front-line Company that had been withdrawn. At about 0330 hour the two Companies around the left road of the "Y" launched a limited attack while the "thinned out" Company on the front lines supported by fire. Then the attacking Companies withdrew quickly carrying their wounded and dead and reoccupied their original defensive positions. The only time during WWII this was done to the best of my knowledge. It worked like a charm. According to a couple Germans we captured later they believed we had been reinforced and now was up to at least Regimental strength.

The following morning (when the Germans were ordered to attack at 0530 and destroy us) I requested our Divisional Artillery to give us a TOT on the German position at 0500. In addition, we hand carried 81 mm mortar ammo all night long. At 0500 All Hell broke loose when we opened up with every available weapon. Later three captured Germans said we decimated them because they were caught out of their fox holes and caught by surprise. At about 0900 we did get an attack supported by tanks but it had no punch.

A couple days later a U.S. Armored Division (I believe the 12th) moved up on our left and blew the only bridge between us.

This was the 2nd Battalion, 8th Infantry Regiment's lonely and memorable defensive stand against the Bulge. I believe the location of the hill mass was Mersch and Echternach was slightly North East and Wallerbilling was further to the North East.

During George L. Mabry Jr.'s service with the 4th Infantry Division, Mabry received the Medal of Honor, the Distinguished Service Cross, the Silver Star, the Bronze Star Medal with V device, the Purple Heart, the Combat Infantry Badge, the Presidential Unit Citation, the European-African-Middle

Eastern Campaign Medal with arrowhead device and three bronze service stars, the American Campaign Medal, the World War II Victory Medal, the Army of Occupation Medal, the British Distinguished Service Order and the Belgian Fourragere.

Mabry commanded 2nd Battalion 8th Infantry at Camp Butner, North Carolina until the 4th Infantry Division was inactivated in 1946. He remained on active duty in the Army and served two tours in Vietnam. He received the Legion of Merit on his first tour in Vietnam in 1966 and the Distinguished Service Medal on his second tour in Vietnam in 1969-1970. He retired as a Major General on August 1, 1975 with 35 years of service.

George L. Mabry died at the age of 72 on July 13, 1990 and is buried at Church of the Holy Cross Cemetery, Stateburg, Sumter County, South Carolina.

LTC Mac Neely on left and George Mabry on right

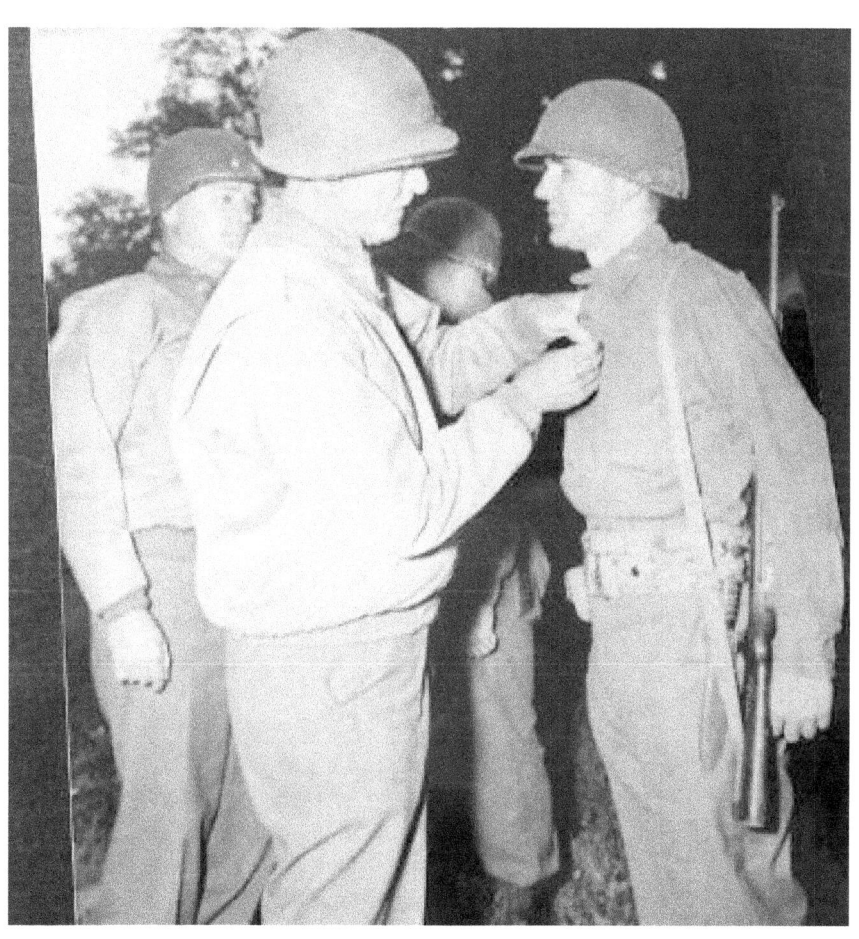

George Mabry receiving Distinguished Service Cross

George Mabry